To anyone who has ever stared at their phone, wallet, or closet and asked, *"What am I doing with my life?"*
This is your wake-up call.
You are not alone. And it is not too late.

THE ULTIMATE AUDIT OF YOUR TIME, ENERGY, AND CHOICES

REALITY CHECK CHRONOS

A FIELD GUIDE TO STOP TRADING YOUR LIFE FOR THINGS YOU DON'T NEED

C. T. JOVENICH

Published by Eco Partner Publishing
Los Angeles, CA
www.ecopartnerpublishing.com

ISBN: 978-1-970285-00-0

Library of Congress Control Number: 2026902608

Disclaimer:
This book is for informational and educational purposes only. It does not constitute medical, legal, financial, or professional advice. The author and publisher make no guarantees regarding outcomes. You are responsible for how you interpret and apply the material.

First edition, 2026
Manufactured in multiple locations worldwide

PREFACE

Your life account is bleeding, and it's not just money.

Let's get real: you're not just spending dollars; you're spending **time**, the only non-renewable resource that truly matters.

We obsess over money, hustle for it, trade our health and energy for it. But money isn't the point, it's just the middleman. The real cost is in minutes, hours, and **heartbeats**.

> This field guide is not a finance manual.
> It's not a productivity hack book.
> **It's your defibrillator, a hard reset.**

We live in a system designed to distract you, drain you, and sell you back a fraction of your own life in the form of dopamine-dusted purchases. If you feel like you're always behind, always tired, always reaching for something just out of frame, **you're not broken.**

You're just in a loop you never designed.

This field guide is the **audit.**
The recalibration.
And the reminder: you can **choose.**

Not someday, **now.**

LOGBOOK

This field guide is yours. Every empty space is intentional.
Use it to think. To question. To plan.
Write in it. Circle. Cross out. Doodle. Do the math.
Fold corners. Highlight what hits. Record reflections.
Sketch ideas. Break patterns.

Chronos is meant to be used, not preserved.

REALITY CHECK: CHRONOS

YOUR JOB'S HIDDEN PRICE TAG

FIELD LOG	SECTOR A1	SEQ: [01/11]

YOUR JOB'S HIDDEN PRICE TAG

Let's expand the lens. This isn't just about math; this is about **meaning**.

You've probably heard someone say, *"Time is money."* **Cute, but here's the truth:** Time is your life. And money is just one way we trade it.

When you're on the job, what you're really doing is trading slices of your existence for currency. And unless you're being paid to do something deeply fulfilling, something aligned with who you are and what matters to you, you may be selling your life at a discount.

Let's call it what it is: wage slavery with a lunch break.

The average person works about 90,000 hours in their lifetime. That's 10.2 years straight, no weekends, no holidays. Would you hand someone a decade of your life in one go and say, *"Do whatever you want with it"*? Didn't think so. But that's essentially the trade we make.

And it gets sneakier. Work doesn't just steal your time. It takes your mornings before you even get there. It shows up in your dreams. It whispers in your mind on Sundays. It makes your shoulders tense when you check your email. This isn't just about hours clocked. **This is about mental rent.**

Let's Go Deeper:

The Invisible Taxes of Employment

I. Commute Cost:

- Fuel, wear and tear, traffic stress, pollution. Add 30 minutes each way? That's 5 hours a week. 20 hours a month. 240 hours a year.

II. Decompression Tax:

- The time it takes to come down from work mode. Some people need an hour of TV, wine, or scrolling to numb out. That's time too.

III. Emotional Drain:

- Toxic coworkers? Soul-sucking meetings. A boss who lives in your head? These are psychic tolls. They don't show up on the paycheck, but they show up in your energy, sleep, relationships, and creativity.

IV. Opportunity Cost:

- What didn't you build? What business did you never start? Which passion project gathered dust because work took the front seat?

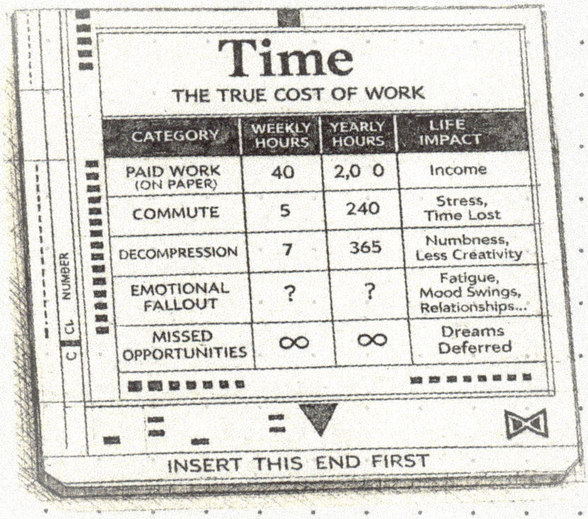

Time

THE TRUE COST OF WORK

CATEGORY	WEEKLY HOURS	YEARLY HOURS	LIFE IMPACT
PAID WORK (ON PAPER)	40	2,0 0	Income
COMMUTE	5	240	Stress, Time Lost
DECOMPRESSION	7	365	Numbness, Less Creativity
EMOTIONAL FALLOUT	?	?	Fatigue, Mood Swings, Relationships...
MISSED OPPORTUNITIES	∞	∞	Dreams Deferred

INSERT THIS END FIRST

Put Pen to Paper:

Your Invisible Tax Worksheet

- How many hours do you spend getting to/from work each week?

→

- How long does it take you to mentally decompress after work?

→

- How often do you think about work on your days off?

→

- When was the last time you chased what excites you?

→

People lose decades avoiding these questions. **Don't be one of them.**

- **Quick Reflection:**

Your Real-Hourly Rate

Most people think in paychecks, not in time.
Every dollar you earn costs slices of your life.
When you count only your work hours, you lie to yourself about the real cost.

Your job doesn't end when you clock out. It follows you home through the commute, the decompression, and the mental bandwidth it occupies.

Translation:
You sell more than work hours.
You sell preparation, recovery, and mental load.
We measure your Real-Hourly Rate to expose your true life-wage.

Let's run the numbers:

Step 1: Monthly Net Pay

→ $ [ ]

Step 2: Total Monthly Hours
Include everything your job consumes in a month:

work hours ____ **commute** ____ **decompression** ____ **mental load** ____

→ For the grand total of [ ] hours

Step 3: Divide Monthly Net Pay by Total Monthly Hours

→ **YOUR REAL-HOURLY RATE IS $ [ ] PER HOUR.**

If it feels low, it's because it is.
That's clarity. And clarity is **leverage**.

- **How does that compare to what you thought?**

→

- **What was the last purchase you made?**

→

- **How many real hours did that last purchase cost you, and was it worth the trade?**
  - You paid the amount of **$** ______
  - Divided by **Step 3**, your Real-Hourly Rate

You've spent ______ **hours** of your life to buy it.

Worth the Trade? ☐ YES ☐ NO

If the cost stings, that's what the truth feels like without filters.

- **Quick Reflection:**

Emotional Audit

Mark the emotions you've felt in the last 30 days on the job:

- ☐ Resentment
- ☐ Pride
- ☐ Burnout
- ☐ Challenge
- ☐ Numbness
- ☐ Growth
- ☐ Drained
- ☐ Energized

- **What would your job need to look like to be worth your time?**

→

To cross from your known universe into the unknown universe, you don't walk; you quantum leap.

Quantum Leap Jumpstart

- **If you renegotiated your entire relationship with work, what becomes possible?**
    - Can you shift to a 4-day workweek? ☐ YES ☐ NO
    - Can you move closer? ☐ YES ☐ NO
    - Can you ask for remote work? ☐ YES ☐ NO
    - Can you transition to freelancing? ☐ YES ☐ NO

- **What can you finally build if you stop waiting?**

☐ **Project 1:**

WHAT FORGOTTEN PROJECTS COME TO MIND?

☐ **Project 2:**

☐ **Project 3:**

☐ **Project 4:**

☐ **Project 5:**

This is where your old life argues with your new one. **Don't bargain.**

QUANTUM LEAPS START BY ASKING BOLDER QUESTIONS.

Let's Do the Math Most People Avoid

Here's a simple example:
Say you earn $100 a day. At first glance, that looks like a win. You picture a crisp Benjamin in your hand at the end of a hard day. But let's unpack what that money really cost you, not in dollars, **but in pieces of your life.**

Let's add it up:

- 8 hours working
- 2 hours of commuting (round trip)
- 1 hour decompressing or worrying about tomorrow
- 0.5 hours getting ready (shower, dress, prepare)

You didn't sell 8 hours for $100. You sold **11.5 hours.**

Your Real-Hourly Rate: $100 ÷ 11.5 = **$8.70/hour**

YOUR JOB DOESN'T JUST TAKE TIME.
IT RESHAPES YOU.

Now look around your house:

- That $120 pair of headphones?
  That's 13.8 hours of your life. **Gone.**

- That fancy new chair? 20 hours.

If your life were a currency, you just spent days on objects that sit idle most of the time. And almost nothing we buy justifies the time we gave up for it.

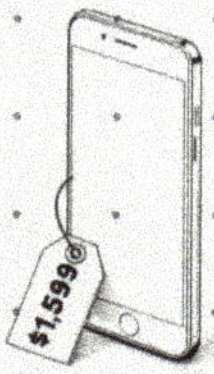

Go deeper into the damage

- Does your job demand emotional labor that drains you?
- Is your work anxiety leaking into your relationships?
- Is recovery time from your job stealing hours from your projects?
- Quick Reflection:

WORK PAYS YOUR BILLS, BUT IT CAN COST YOUR PEACE.

Put Pen to Paper: Life-Wage Reality Check

Step 1: Calculate your Real-Hourly Rate

- Use your actual Real-Hourly Rate calculation [006.3]

→ $ ______ per Hour

Step 2: Audit your last 5 purchases

- How many real work hours did you trade for each one?

Items	Price	Hours Traded	Worth it?
1.			☐ YES ☐ NO
2.			☐ YES ☐ NO
3.			☐ YES ☐ NO
4.			☐ YES ☐ NO
5.			☐ YES ☐ NO

Quantum Leap Jumpstart

What changes when you stop treating your job as a money machine and start seeing it as a life-exchange terminal?

- **How does that shift what you're willing to work for?**

→

- **What purchases stop making sense when you measure the cost in life instead of money?**

→

IF YOU WOULDN'T TRADE AN ACTUAL DAY OF YOUR LIFE FOR IT, DON'T BUY IT.

Put Pen to Paper:

Redesign Your Work Life

- **Which parts of your work day drain you the most, and why?**

→

- **What does your ideal 4-hour workday look like?**

→

- **What's one action that gets you 5% closer this month?**

→

5% SHIFTS DIRECTION.
DIRECTION CHANGES EVERYTHING.

Put Pen to Paper:

The Life Trade Ledger

- Track where your time and energy are really going, hour by hour, trade by trade.
- For every activity, log the time spent, the value gained, and the emotional cost.
- Did it energize you or drain you? Fulfill you or frustrate you?
- This isn't just about productivity. It's about **alignment.**
- The goal? Spot the time drains. Catch the emotional leaks. **Reclaim your life.**

Task / Commitment	Hours/Week	Emotional Cost	Is it Worth It?
			☐ YES ☐ NO
			☐ YES ☐ NO
			☐ YES ☐ NO
			☐ YES ☐ NO
			☐ YES ☐ NO
			☐ YES ☐ NO
			☐ YES ☐ NO
			☐ YES ☐ NO
			☐ YES ☐ NO
			☐ YES ☐ NO
			☐ YES ☐ NO

Time Drains = obligations and interruptions that quietly siphon your life, unchallenged.

- **What can you stop doing this month to get 5 hours of your life back?**

→

MONEY IS TEMPORARY AND TIME DOESN'T RESET.

- **What could you start doing with that time?**

→

Most people wait until burnout to answer these questions. **You don't have to.**

A Global Lens:
Not Everyone Buys the Same Lie

Zoom out.

The hustle script isn't universal. It's a U.S. export, where your job becomes your identity, output becomes your worth, and marketing algorithms stalk your attention 24/7. But the rest of the world doesn't always play by that script.

In France:

- Workweeks are legally capped at 35 hours. Vacations? Mandatory, and people actually take them. Entire cities pause in August. Long lunches with friends aren't indulgent; they're expected.

In Japan:

- Overwork is rampant (a cautionary tale) to the point that *karōshi* means "death by overwork." But there's a deep cultural reverence for discipline, beauty, and the collective good. Rituals like tea ceremonies and forest bathing serve as spiritual counterweights offered not as escape, but as restoration.

In Argentina:

- Community time is sacred. Sundays mean family *asados*, not inboxes. Yerba mate isn't rushed; it's shared. And in many towns, slowing down in the afternoon is part of the rhythm.

In Denmark:

- *Hygge* is a way of life, comfort, togetherness, and contentment. It's not a brand; it's cultural DNA. Denmark consistently ranks high in happiness and work-life balance. The social system supports people with healthcare, parental leave, unemployment benefits, and strong worker protections.

What's the common thread?

These cultures have, to varying degrees, created norms that resist total colonization by consumerism and hustle culture. Not perfectly; but enough to prove there are other ways to live.

- **Quick Reflection:**

EVERY HOUR SPENT SHOULD FEED YOUR SPIRIT, NOT JUST YOUR SCHEDULE.

Decision Matrix: "Stay or Shift?"

1.	Do I feel proud of how I spend my weekdays?	☐ YES	☐ NO
2.	Would I still do this job if money weren't an issue?	☐ YES	☐ NO
3.	Does this job align with my core values?	☐ YES	☐ NO
4.	Do I feel energized when I show up for work?	☐ YES	☐ NO
5.	Do I feel respected, safe, and seen?	☐ YES	☐ NO

Score: If you answered *"No"* at least 3 times, it's time to explore a **shift**.

Journal: A Letter to My Current Job

Write the letter you've been editing in your head. Thank it for what it's given you. Admit what it's taken. Question what it's costing. Let the truth come out. You don't have to send it. **Just write.**

→

THE JOB ISN'T THE VILLAIN. AUTOPILOT IS.

Declaration: Claim Your Life Back

This is your moment to draw the line. To name what's yours, what you're done sacrificing and what you're ready to reclaim.

→

"I am not just my resume. I am not my output.
I am not a machine built to perform.
My life is mine. My time is mine.
And I will choose how I spend it.

X_______________

Sign it. Date it. Tape it to your mirror.

Read this declaration aloud. Let it be your reset, your cue to stop living on autopilot and **start living by design.**

THIS PAGE MARKS THE LINE. DON'T STEP BACK.
FROM HERE ON, YOU CHOOSE.

- **Field Log [A1] Reflections:**

REALITY CHECK: CHRONOS

THE CLOCK DOESN'T LIE

FIELD LOG	SECTOR B2	SEQ: [02/11]

THE CLOCK DOESN'T LIE

Time isn't just a number. It's the currency of life, paid out second by second. It doesn't get saved. It doesn't get refunded. And it doesn't wait for us to get our act together.

Every breath is an investment. Every choice is a transaction. You're either buying distraction or direction.

So take a brutally honest inventory:
Assume, optimistically, you'll live to age 100. If you're 46 now, that gives you 54 years left.

That equals:

- **19,726 days** (including leap years)
- **473,424 total hours**

Now subtract sleep (8 hours per day):
8 × 19,726 = 157,808 hours asleep

Leaving you with approximately **315,616 waking hours.**
But not all of that time is truly free.

Now subtract time spent on:
eating, grooming, errands, cleaning, waiting, commuting, doomscrolling, buffering through burnout, decision fatigue, low energy, anxiety, chores, maintenance, taxes, laundry, leaks, and all the small frictions of daily life.

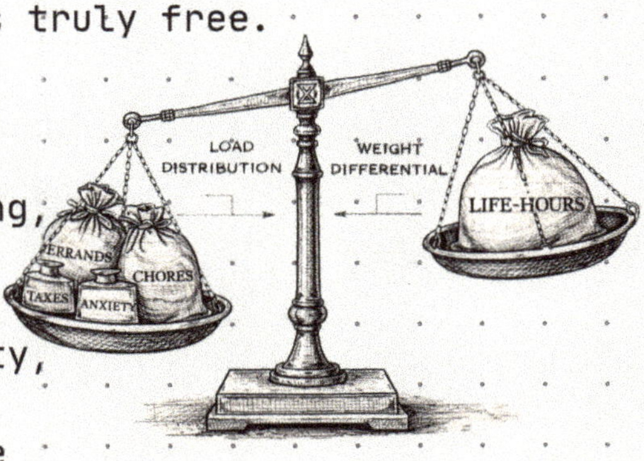

A conservative estimate? You'll lose half of that to required survival mode.

That leaves you with: 157,808 usable hours... and likely less, depending on your lifestyle.

But it's not just a bad trade. it's a machine.

Advertising doesn't just sell you things. It sells you identities. Every logo, every ad, every influencer haul whispers the same command: *buy this, become this, be seen.*

Even the "freedom" products like minimalism, decluttering, and simplicity all get turned into merch. Try to step outside the system and it packages the exit and sells it back to you.

And while you chase what they dangle, the meter keeps running. You don't just lose money. You lose the only currency you can never earn back.

The psychology underneath it:

- **Decision fatigue:** too many choices drain your clarity.
- **Temporal discounting:** the brain chases now, even when later is the real win.
- **Peak-hour bias:** you only get a few windows each day when your mind is at full strength.

Your brain burns 20–25% of your energy every day. Every extra decision steals fuel. That's why doomscrolling hits harder at night. By then, **you're empty.**

Put Pen to Paper:

Usable Time Audit Reality Check

Fill in the blanks. Show your math in the margins.

Your **age**: ______

Expected **lifespan**: ______

(Average U.S.: Men ≈ 73.5 years | Women ≈ 79.3 years)

Remaining **years**: (lifespan - age) ______

Remaining **days**: (years x 365) ______

Remaining **hours**: (days x 24) ______

−

Hours lost to **sleep**: (days x 8) ______

\+

Hours lost to **maintenance**: (days x 5) ______

(eating / hygiene / chores)

REAL LIFE-HOURS REMAINING: = ______

(remaining hours - sleep - maintenance)

↑ THIS MAY BE ALL THE TIME YOU HAVE LEFT TO TRULY LIVE.

Quantum Leap Jumpstart

- **What's one thing you keep telling yourself you'll do... but don't?**

→

- **What excuses have you used to avoid doing it?**

→

Imagine doing it once. What would that feel like?

Make Your Non-Negotiable List Of Life Experiences You Refuse To Miss

→

IF YOUR SCHEDULE DOESN'T MATCH YOUR VALUES, YOUR LIFE WON'T EITHER.

Quantum Leap Jumpstart

Look back at your list. Time won't wait.

- **Which of these can you start or move forward this week?**

→

The Compound Effect of Small Choices

- **Let's say you waste just 1 hour a day:**
  - That's 365 hours a year.
  - 15 full days.
  - About 380 days; a whole year across 25.

Flip it. Spend that same hour reading, walking, learning, connecting. **Quietly. Powerfully. Irrevocably.**

THIS IS WHERE YOUR LIFE UPGRADES.

- **What's one hour you could invest each day that would change your life in five years?**

→

- **Now double it. What happens if you give it two?**

→

Time Debt vs. Time Wealth

If you spend your best hours on survival and distraction, you're in **time debt.** If you invest your peak hours in alignment, love, and legacy, you're building **time wealth.**

- **Where are you right now?**

☐ Debt ☐ Break-even ☐ Building wealth

- **How do you want that answer to change?**

→

TIME DEBT COLLECTS COMPOUNDED REGRET.

Leadership by Example

For years, I didn't just talk about these ideas, I lived them. By helping my teams focus not just on hard skills like closing deals and hitting numbers, but on soft skills like presence, mindset, reflection, and emotional discipline, and with it, I helped reshape how clean energy sales teams were built.

For over 10 years, at three of the nation's leading renewable energy companies, we didn't just build top-performing teams, we built the **happiest.** The most **resilient.** The most **real.**
Our numbers were record-breaking, yes but more importantly, so were our relationships, our mental health, and our joy.

Why? Because we worked to **live.** Not the other way around.

Quantum Leap Jumpstart

Start the clock: today is where the shift begins.

- **Set Your Intention:** I will reclaim ______ hours a week from distractions

- **I will reinvest them into:**

→

The Time Autopsy

- Yesterday I spent my time on:
  - ☐ Morning: →
  - ☐ Midday: →
  - ☐ Evening: →
- Unconscious habits:

→

- What would a better day actually look like?

→

YOUR FIRST STEP OUTWEIGHS EVERY MOMENT OF INDECISION.

A Global Lens:
Not All Clocks Tick the Same

We work to live. We don't live to work.

That simple truth, so easy to say, so hard to embody, is the dividing line between **burnout** and **balance.**

In many parts of the world, time isn't sliced and monetized the way it is in the U.S. **And it's worth asking:** What if the issue isn't how much time we have, but the culture teaching us how to use it?

Let's zoom out again.
Time is experienced differently across the globe:

🇮🇹 **In Italy:**

- *La dolce vita* isn't just a phrase, it's a tempo. Meals last hours, schedules bend around joy, and pausing is part of the plan.

🇮🇳 **In India:**

- Time isn't always linear. In many parts of India, people live by what's jokingly called "Indian Stretchable Time," flexible and fluid. Priorities shift. Human connection often comes before the clock.

🇸🇪 **In Sweden:**

- Lagom, not too much, not too little, applies to time, too. There's a cultural lean toward balance, moderation, and work-life harmony.

What's the Common Thread? These cultures move to different rhythms, but they share a deeper wisdom. Time isn't just measured in minutes, it's measured in **meaning.**

Across the world, the most memorable moments aren't rushed.
They are stretched, savored, and lived fully, reminding us that real living happens between the ticks of the clock.

Compare This To The American Grind

- Urgency is glorified.
- Schedules are stacked.
- Busyness = virtue.
- Downtime = guilt.

But living like a spinning top doesn't mean you're progressing. It just means you're **dizzy**.

The Illusion of "Later"

The average adult says *"I'll get to it later"* about 7–10 times a day:

- Later becomes next week.
- Next week becomes next year.
- And then someday never comes.

Let's replace "later" with:

- *"Not a priority right now."*
- *"I'm afraid to begin."*
- *"I don't know where to start."*

Because **clarity** kills excuses.

- **Quick Reflection:**

"TOMORROW" STEALS MORE DREAMS THAN FAILURE WILL EVER DO.

Put Pen to Paper:

The Day Swap Exercise

Divide the page in half.

On the left: list the key pieces of your average day. Not every detail, just the largest blocks that define how your time is spent, for example: work, commute, meals, screen time, rest.

On the right: sketch the key pieces of your ideal day. Focus on structure and flow, not perfection.

What does an aligned daily rhythm look like?

AVERAGE DAY	IDEAL DAY
→	→

- **Ask yourself:**
  - Which elements from the right side can you implement tomorrow?
  - What's the most draining part of your current day?
  - What's one small change you can make today to move toward the ideal?

A **time revolution** begins with **one deliberate choice.**

The Daily Investment Tracker (Use Weekly)

(e.g., breathwork, journaling, or a walk).

Activity	Joy Level (1-10)	Growth?	Keep Doing?
		☐ YES ☐ NO	☐ YES ☐ NO
		☐ YES ☐ NO	☐ YES ☐ NO
		☐ YES ☐ NO	☐ YES ☐ NO
		☐ YES ☐ NO	☐ YES ☐ NO
		☐ YES ☐ NO	☐ YES ☐ NO
		☐ YES ☐ NO	☐ YES ☐ NO
		☐ YES ☐ NO	☐ YES ☐ NO

Quantum Leap Jumpstart

- **What's one thing I'll stop giving my time to this week?**

→

- **What is one thing I will start saying yes to, even in small doses?**

→

- **If I only had 3 years left, what would I instantly stop tolerating?**

→

- **If my time was worth $1,000/hour, would I spend it the same way?**

→

THE PAST IS GONE. ONLY NOW HOLDS POWER.

Deep Dive: What is Time?

- **Augustine of Hippo (354 to 430 CE, Roman North Africa)**

Time lives inside the mind as memory and expectation. Augustine described the past as recollection and the future as anticipation. He argued that time is not something we stand outside of. We carry it. What we call time is stitched from what we remember and what we imagine next.

FIG. 1. ST. AUGUSTINE

- **Lucius Annaeus Seneca (4 BCE–65 CE, Roman Empire)**

Mortality gives weight to every hour. Seneca believed that awareness of death sharpens existence. A finite life demands decisions. Each moment matters because it cannot return. Urgency is not panic. It is clarity born from limits.

Fig. 2. Lucius Annaeus Seneca

- **Jean-Paul Sartre (1905-1980, France)**

Freedom happens inside time. Sartre argued that every moment presents a choice, and those choices accumulate into identity. We are not defined once. We are defined continuously. Time is the medium where responsibility lives.

FIG. 3. JEAN-PAUL SARTRE

Whether you see time as a countdown, a cycle, or a field of possibilities, your definition shapes your strategy. If Life-Hours are your only currency, philosophy stops being abstract. It becomes **financial planning for existence.**

- **Field Log [B2] Reflections:**

REALITY CHECK: CHRONOS

TOO MUCH STUFF, TOO LITTLE LIFE

FIELD LOG	SECTOR C3	SEQ: [03/11]

TOO MUCH STUFF, TOO LITTLE LIFE

Let's be honest: most of us are drowning in things. Closets full of clothes we don't wear. Shelves stacked with stuff we forgot we owned. Digital folders bursting with files, photos, and promises we'll *"get to eventually."* And garages? They've become graveyards of hobbies we never followed through on.

The Heavy Cost of "More"

Stuff doesn't just take space; it drains energy, attention, maintenance, and Life-Hours.
You buy it, store it, clean it, repair it, reorganize it, feel guilty about it, and eventually get overwhelmed by it.

We're living in an era where possessions multiply faster than **meaning.** The average American household owns tens of thousands of items. And still, we feel like something's missing.

WE USED TO OWN THINGS.
NOW THINGS OWN US.

Where This All Comes From

Spoiler: it's **not** your fault. But it is **your** responsibility.

We're raised inside a machine that runs on consumption. From childhood, we're told that success looks like a bigger house, a newer car, and the latest phone. We're bombarded with thousands of ads per day. Every app, every website, every scroll is a pitch.

We're taught that if we're feeling low, buying something will fix it. If we feel insecure, we're told dressing "right," whatever that means, will help. If we're bored, a new gadget or box delivered to our door will lift us.
And for a moment? It often works. You get a dopamine hit. You feel seen. You feel excited. Until that shiny new thing becomes part of the **clutter**.

Welcome to the consumption hangover:

- **The Consumption Dopamine Cycle**
  - Anticipation hits harder than ownership.
- **Adaptation cycle**
  - Your brain adapts quickly, gets bored fast, which is why clutter grows.
- **The "Object Guilt Loop"**
  - Avoiding unused items quietly adds stress.

- **Buying triggers dopamine.**
- **Owning triggers maintenance.**
- **Letting go, triggers relief.**

Put Pen to Paper:

Stuff Audit (Part 1)

Pick one room in your home.

Then:

- **Count how many items you've purchased in the last 12 months:**

→

- **Now count how many of those you actually use regularly:**

→

- **What percentage of those purchases felt worth it in hindsight?**

0% **NOT WORTH IT** — **100%** **WORTH IT**

- **How much did you spend total?**

→ $

- **How many Life-Hours was that?**

(Total spent ÷ your Real-Hourly Rate) [006.3]

→ Life-Hours

Pause.
This isn't about blame. It's about clarity, and what you do with it.

YOU DIDN'T BUILD THE MACHINE, BUT YOU GET TO BREAK THE CYCLE.

Put Pen to Paper:

Stuff Audit (Part 2)

Let's take it further. This is where the math meets the meaning.

Go to one room in your home, wherever feels the most "stuffed."
Choose 5–10 items you've kept but rarely use.

Item	Estimated Cost	Life-Hour Cost	Still Brings Value?	If Not, Why Keep It?
1.			☐ YES ☐ NO	
2.			☐ YES ☐ NO	
3.			☐ YES ☐ NO	
4.			☐ YES ☐ NO	
5.			☐ YES ☐ NO	
6.			☐ YES ☐ NO	
7.			☐ YES ☐ NO	
8.			☐ YES ☐ NO	
9.			☐ YES ☐ NO	
10.			☐ YES ☐ NO	

- **Quick Reflection:**

- **How did this space feel before this audit?**

→

- **How does it feel now, even just noticing?**

→

- **What are you ready to release this week?**

→

- **What could take its place (peace, space, sunlight, clarity)?**

→

You're not *"getting rid of stuff."* You're reclaiming the Life-Hours you gave to things that stopped serving you.

LETTING GO ISN'T FAILURE, IT'S WISDOM.
IT'S KNOWING WHAT NO LONGER DESERVES YOUR ENERGY.

Here's why it matters

We often frame decluttering as a chore. Something shameful. A reaction to having "too much."

Decluttering isn't about guilt. It's about facing what your things actually cost you.

Everything you own took time to acquire. Every object in your space represents Life-Hours, time you spent working, earning, deciding, shopping, cleaning, maintaining, and sometimes worrying.

That shirt you never wear? It cost you more than money. **It cost you moments of your life you'll never get back.**

Ownership is Energy

Objects don't just take space. They take attention.

- **They whisper:**
    - *"I should use this more."*
    - *"I'll fix that someday."*
    - *"Maybe I'll need it later."*

Each whisper is a micro-drain on your clarity and focus.
Letting go is not loss. It's **liberation.**
When you release what no longer serves you, you're not discarding value. You're reclaiming it.

- **You're saying:**
    - *"I honor the time I spent."*
    - *"I learned from this."*
    - *"I choose not to spend more of my life maintaining what no longer matters."*

You're Entering into a New Agreement

Decluttering isn't just a cleaning task, it's a conscious contract.
You're not just removing items; you're renegotiating the energy in your environment.

- **Every object you release is a statement:**
    - *"I no longer need this version of me."*
    - *"I choose space over stagnation."*
    - *"I trust that letting go creates room for something better."*

This is an energetic realignment, between you, your environment, and your **future**.

You're not downsizing. You're **optimizing**.
You're not discarding the past. You're **designing** your present.

- **This new agreement is subtle, but powerful:**
    - Less noise. More clarity.
    - Less clutter. More creativity.
    - Less guilt. More grace.

You are choosing to fill your space not with more, but with **meaning**.

When you remove an object, you make room for calm, creativity, sunlight, ease, flow.

This isn't subtraction. It's a conscious trade.
You're trading old decisions for new possibilities.

Stuff is about the past.
Space is about the **present**.

Clutter often reflects past versions of you:
Past hobbies, habits, identities.

- **Releasing clutter is saying:**
  - *"I no longer need to carry the past to live my future."*

The Mental Weight of Physical Clutter

Your brain is a pattern recognition machine.
Clutter creates chaos.

- **Every visible item is a micro-decision:**
  - *Should I move this?*
  - *Do I need this?*
  - *Should I throw it out?*

The result? Background stress.
According to neuroscience, physical clutter increases cortisol levels, reduces focus, and drains mental energy.

Translation: clutter strains your brain all day.

Emotional Clutter Is Just as Real

- Clothes that no longer fit = **shame**
- Gifts we don't like but keep = **guilt**
- Projects we abandoned = **regret**

We're not just holding onto things,
we're holding onto identities
we no longer live inside of.
Sit with that for a moment.

Every object you keep either
supports your life or **subtracts** from it.

It's not just your home that gets messy. You feel it in your chest. In your gut. In your throat.

YOU'RE NOT LOSING THINGS.
YOU'RE UPGRADING YOUR ENVIRONMENT.

Clutter Cost Matrix

Type of Clutter	Cost Type	Hidden Effect
physical	space, time	stress, lost time, distraction
digital	mental capacity	overwhelm, disorganization
emotional	energy, identity	guilt, inertia, avoidance
financial	money, Life-Hours	debt, anxiety, scarcity mindset

Minimalism Isn't the Point

It's about being **intentional.**

You don't need to fit your life into a single suitcase. You just need to become someone who knows the difference between what you own and what owns you.

Reclaim that power. ← NO ONE ELSE CAN DO THIS FOR YOU

- **In the next section, we'll walk through:**
  - a full-room decluttering process
  - the digital declutter
  - emotional detachment strategies
  - creating your personal definition of enough

Because shedding stuff isn't just about space. It's about stepping into a version of yourself that's lighter, freer, and finally aligned.

YOU'RE NOT JUST CLEARING SPACE.
YOU'RE GIVING YOUR FUTURE SELF SOMEWHERE TO STAND.

The Physical Declutter: A Room-by-Room Reboot

Start with one space. Any space. Just not your entire house. Trying to declutter everything at once is a recipe for burnout and decision fatigue.

Decluttering Protocol:

A — CHOOSE ONE SPACE

This is not a lifestyle overhaul. It's a single decision. One room. One boundary. One clear win. Finish it.

KITCHEN

CLOSET

BEDROOM

GARAGE

B — SET A TIMER

45 minutes of focused effort beats 3 hours of distracted work. Timebox the session to protect clarity and avoid decision fatigue.
When the timer ends, you stop. Even if you're not done. This protects energy and keeps tomorrow's motivation intact.

- **Momentum comes from finishing, not starting big.**
- **Consistency beats intensity, every time.**

Decluttering Execution Sheet

Time	45-Min Tasks	15-Min Reset
6:00 AM		☐
7:00 AM		☐
8:00 AM		☐
9:00 AM		☐
10:00 AM		☐
11:00 AM		☐
12:00 PM	**LUNCH BREAK**	
1:00 PM		
2:00 PM		☐
3:00 PM		☐
4:00 PM		☐
5:00 PM		☐
6:00 PM		☐
7:00 PM	**STOP, RECAP AND RESET**	
8:00 PM		

Focus Level of the Day: 1 | 2 | 3 | 4 | 5 | 6 | 7 | 8 | 9 | 10

Not all hours are equal. Plan around energy, not willpower. Two rules of engagement: finish what you start, and don't burn out.

- **Quick Reflection:**

C USE THE 4-BOX METHOD

- Label four boxes (or corners) clearly.
- Gather your tools, a marker, four boxes, trash bags, and clean containers for items you keep.
- Set up a clear workspace so you can sort everything quickly.

KEEP
Love it, use it, need it

DONATE
Good shape, not for you

TRASH
Broken, expired, or beyond repair

RELOCATE
Belongs somewhere else

DON'T LET YOUR GARAGE BECOME A DUMPING GROUND!

D ASK THESE 3 QUESTIONS

1. Do I use it regularly?
2. Do I love it?
3. Would I buy it again at full price today?

If the answer is NO to all three, **LET IT GO.**

DON'T JUST ORGANIZE YOUR CHAOS. ELIMINATE IT.

What This Audit Reveals

- You don't wear half your clothes
- You're storing broken gadgets "just in case"
- You own duplicates of the same tools, chargers, notebooks, or containers
- You're holding guilt-linked clutter (gifts, inherited items, hobbies you gave up)

Put Pen to Paper:

Physical Inventory Worksheet

Start with the first items that come to mind.

Item	Love It?	Would Rebuy?	Keep or Release?
	☐ YES ☐ NO	☐ YES ☐ NO	☐ K ☐ R
	☐ YES ☐ NO	☐ YES ☐ NO	☐ K ☐ R
	☐ YES ☐ NO	☐ YES ☐ NO	☐ K ☐ R
	☐ YES ☐ NO	☐ YES ☐ NO	☐ K ☐ R

- **How did it feel letting something go?**

→

- **What emotion came up? Relief? Guilt? Excitement?**

→

AWARENESS IS YOUR REBELLION.
LIBERATION IS YOUR REVOLUTION.

The Digital Declutter

Clutter isn't just physical. Every open tab, email notification, or scattered folder on your desktop pulls at your attention.

You wouldn't let 300 people shout at you every morning, but that's what your inbox is doing.

- **What do you feel every time you open your inbox?**

→

Areas to Declutter

- **Email** (Unsubscribe. Archive. Delete.)
- **Photos** (Remove duplicates, screenshots, accidental captures)
- **Files** (Delete or organize unused documents)
- **Apps** (Remove anything unused in 30 days)
- **Notifications** (Turn off everything nonessential)

BRING PATIENCE. THIS TAKES LONGER THAN YOU THINK.

Recommended Flow

1. Email Audit: Start by deleting promotional junk. Then mass-archive everything older than 90 days.

2. Folder Structure: Create 3 to 5 master folders. Keep it simple.

3. Photos: Use your phone's "Duplicates" feature to mass-merge or delete once a week. Do the same on any connected cloud photo services for a full digital cleanup.

4. App Detox: Which apps drain you the most? List them:

→

Digital Declutter Tracker

Area	Action Needed	Completed
email	archive, delete, unsubscribe	☐
photos	delete duplicates	☐
files	sort and label	☐
apps	remove unused	☐
notifications	turn off nonessential	☐

- **What's one digital change that instantly made your mind feel lighter?**

→

Special Focus: Forgotten Media, Forgotten Time

Let's talk about books, CDs, DVDs, VHS tapes, and even cassette tapes still living in boxes in your garage or hallway closet.

We tell ourselves they're special. And maybe they are. But when's the last time you listened to that mix CD from 2003? Watched that still-wrapped box set of a show you swore you'd binge *"someday"*?

Books we'll *"definitely read"* one day? That day rarely comes. But the guilt of not reading them sits like dust in the corners of your consciousness.

This is common. Most of us own more media than we'll ever consume. And while physical media had a golden age, it's okay to admit you've moved on. Letting go doesn't mean erasing memory, it means choosing space for what matters **now**.

Your attention is limited. Don't let a box of nostalgia take priority over peace.

Let It Go Ideas:

- **Donate** books to a local free library.
- **Digitize** your CDs and tapes if you want, then recycle them.
- **Keep** one symbolic DVD or VHS tape, let the rest go.

Let's Talk Clothes, Shoes, and Bags

Closets are shrines to past identities:

- The body we used to have
- The fantasy life we never quite lived
- The style we hoped to pull off

It's time for a reality check in your wardrobe.

If it doesn't fit, you don't use it, or it drags your energy down, **it's time to let it go.**

Ditch impulse buys and anything that doesn't fit. Try it on. If it doesn't fit, it doesn't belong.

Too much clothing? Donate it. Giving feels better than storing guilt.

Get rid of unworn shoes, old purses, uniforms, and branded clothing. Don't be a walking billboard.

Let go of at least 5 items per category.

Easier Goodbyes:

- Host a clothing swap with friends
- Sell higher-end items online
- Create a capsule wardrobe: 30-40 items that mix and match with ease

Every piece of clothing you keep should say:

"I belong in your future."

The Cleaning Supply Graveyard

Check under your sink. In your laundry room. In your garage.
There's likely an army of barely-used sprays, scrubs, waxes, and tools you bought in a moment of motivation or marketing hypnosis.

Now they just take up shelf space and psychic space. Half-empty bottles of "miracle degreaser," Replacement parts for things you no longer have, and cleaning gadgets with four different attachments you never learned to use.

Let them go. They're not making you cleaner; they're cluttering your resolve.

Tip: Pick one all-purpose cleaner that works well. Ditch the rest.

The Collector's Trap: When Identity Becomes Inventory

Collecting can be beautiful. Ritualistic. Personal. But there's a fine line between curation and compulsion.
Some say they collect vintage tins, whiskey bottles, branded cups, candles, figurines, or enamel pins. But if the collection lives in a box you never open, or it overwhelms your space, what is it actually **adding** to your life?

Collectors vs. Accumulators:

Question	Collector's Response	Accumulators' Behavior
is it curated and intentional?	yes	no, random accumulation
is it displayed or stored?	displayed and rotated	packed away and forgotten
does it bring joy?	yes	guilt or stress
is there a plan for it?	yes, displayed or used	no, fear of letting go

POSSESSIONS

Be honest: are you collecting or avoiding letting go?

- **Quick Reflection:**

A COLLECTION SHOULD ADD BEAUTY, MEANING, OR DELIGHT, NOT DUST.

Practices for Letting Go Emotionally

Say It Out Loud

- *"I am no longer that person."*
- *"I don't need to finish this to prove my worth."*
- *"This belonged to a chapter that's now complete."*

Write a Goodbye Letter

- You don't need to mail it.
- Just write it.
- Say goodbye to the story or identity tied to the object.

Forgive Yourself

- You did the best you could with who you were, what you had, and what you knew at the time. Let that be enough.

Put Pen to Paper:

Emotional Object Audit

Item/Memory	Emotion It Carries	Still Serves You?	Keep or Release?
		□ YES □ NO	□ K □ R
		□ YES □ NO	□ K □ R
		□ YES □ NO	□ K □ R
		□ YES □ NO	□ K □ R
		□ YES □ NO	□ K □ R

- **What's the most emotionally heavy object you've been holding on to?**

→

- **Why have you kept it?**

→

- **How would it feel to let it go?**

→

- **Quick Reflection:**

Redefining "Enough"

Before you define enough, understand this:
The emotional high lives in the wanting. The moment you get the thing, the spike fades. Soon it blends into the background. What felt urgent becomes ordinary.
If you don't define enough, you'll keep chasing the next spike.

"ENOUGH" IS A MOVING TARGET
BUT ONLY YOU SHOULD DECIDE WHERE IT MOVES.

How do you know when you have enough? If you never stop to define that line, the world will gladly keep selling to you until you're broke, exhausted, and buried.

Enough isn't minimal. It's **intentional.**

Define Your Enough:

- How many pairs of shoes do you need?
- How many streaming subscriptions?
- How much wall space do you want filled?
- How many plates do you actually use?

There's no magic number. There's just **clarity**.

Create Your Enough List

Start with these three categories. Define what enough means for you.
When you're done, add one new category at a time.

Example:

- **Clothes:** Enough is about 40 items total, all worn regularly
- **Books:** Enough is one unread shelf at a time
- **Tech:** Enough is one phone, one laptop, no tablets gathering dust

Your Turn:

- **Clothes:** →
- **Books:** →
- **Tech:** →
- **Pick a new category (repeat as needed):**

→

How Experiences Create Real Value

Now that you've made space, we move to what you choose to fill it with: **experiences.**

Things that don't sit on a shelf, but live in your memory, shape your character, and stretch your capacity to feel alive.

Let's be clear: the opposite of clutter isn't minimalism. It's meaning.

When you trade Life-Hours for something physical, you get an object. When you trade Life-Hours for an experience, you get a memory, a story, and often a deeper version of yourself.

Experiences shape identity. They shift perspective. They plant moments of wonder, courage, and connection into the timeline of your life.

That $200 trip stays with you. That $200 chair fades from your mind the moment it gets scratched.

- **Moments** become cherished memories.
- **Relationships** deepen through shared experiences.
- **Perspectives** expand when we step outside our routine.

• **Quick Reflection:**

EXPERIENCES DON'T SIT ON SHELVES. THEY STAY ALIVE IN YOU.

A Life-Hours Comparison: Experience vs. Possession

Purchase	Cost in Life-Hours	Outcome
designer shoes	12 hours	occasional use, guilt later
weekend camping trip	12 hours	laughter, peace, connection
new tablet (3rd one)	16 hours	convenience, more screen time
dance class + dinner date	16 hours	growth, intimacy, fun

Memory Dividends: The ROI of Moments

- An adventure you tell for years.
- A moment of awe that shifts your worldview.
- A meal with someone who is now gone.
- A class that changes how you see your body or mind.

These moments don't depreciate. **They compound.**

Quantum Leap Jumpstart

- **What is an experience you've been putting off?**

→

- **What's one step you could take this week to move toward it?**

→

- **If you knew you had 2 years to live, would you make it happen?** ☐ YES ☐ NO ☐ NOT SURE

BECOME THE ARCHITECT OF YOUR LIFE:
LIVE ON PURPOSE. SET YOUR SOUL ON FIRE.

Put Pen to Paper:

Experience Wish List

List 10 experiences that would light you up. Big or small.

1.

2.

3.

4.

5.

6.

7.

8.

9.

10.

Highlight 3. Act on 1 this week. Put a date on it.

If you're going to spend your Life-Hours, spend them on something that gives you life back.

- **Field Log [C3] Reflections:**

REALITY CHECK: CHRONOS

EXPERIENCES BEAT CLUTTER

FIELD LOG	SECTOR D4	SEQ: [04/11]

EXPERIENCES BEAT CLUTTER

We live in a world where most people are starving for experiences and stuffed with things. And we wonder why we feel unfulfilled.

This chapter flips that equation. It shifts your focus from possession to participation, from accumulation to engagement.

You don't need more stuff. You need more moments that stick to your soul, not just your shelves.

Why Experiences Matter

- **They build identity:** they change you.
- **They carry emotion:** they move you.
- **They are time-bound:** they demand presence.
- **They create connection:** they are rarely lived alone.

Possessions require upkeep.
Experiences stay with you.

THE JOY OF THINGS FADES AS THEY SIT.

THE JOY OF EXPERIENCES GROWS AS YOU RETELL.

The Neuroscience of Experience

Your brain tends to remember what carries emotional weight. A trip, a performance, a hike, a concert.

Moments like these activate dopamine, serotonin, and adrenaline, the chemicals that help experiences feel vivid and meaningful.

- Buying gives a temporary chemical high.
- Experiences create a longer-lasting one.

This isn't just psychology. It's **chemistry.**

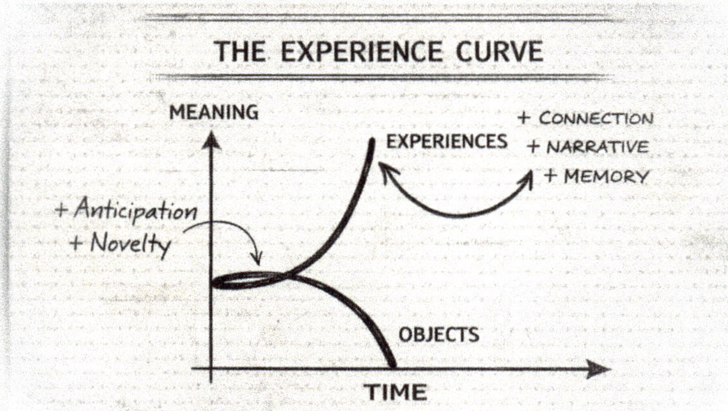

The Experience Quotient

Let's start measuring differently. Instead of net worth, what about **net wonder**?

Ask yourself:

- How many stories can I tell from the past six months?
- When was the last time I felt fully immersed in something?
- When did I last do something that stretched me beyond my comfort zone?

The more alive you feel, the less you'll look to things to fill the gap.

Designing a Life Full of Experience

How do you build a life rich in moments instead of materials?

You don't need to travel the world or spend a fortune. **You need intention.**

The Ingredients of a Rich Experience

- **Novelty:** Do something new.
- **Emotion:** Engage your heart, not just your eyes.
- **Presence:** Be fully in the moment.
- **Meaning:** Choose experiences aligned with your values.
- **People:** Share it, or be deeply present with yourself.

Most people drift into experiences by accident.

Design yours on purpose.

TIME GIVES YOU MINUTES. RITUAL MAKES THEM MEMORABLE.

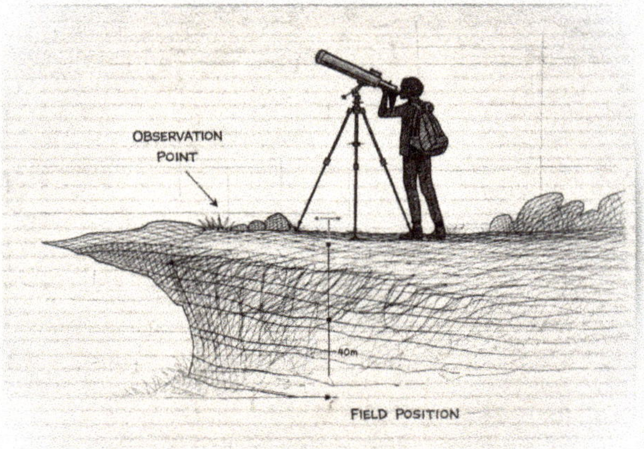

- **Quick Reflection:**

Experience Menu: Micro to Macro

Type	Cost	Time Required	Impact Potential
watch sunrise solo	free	30 min	calm, awe, reflection
take a day trip	low	4-12 hours	exploration, novelty
try a new cuisine	medium	2 hours	sensory delight, culture
take a class	varies	weekly	skill growth, confidence
book a retreat	high	2-7 days	life-changing perspective

Start small. Schedule one experience a week.
Put it on your calendar.

Your Experience Map

On the next pages, begin three lists:

- **Daily Moments:** Small experiences, 5-30 minutes, that make life feel fuller.
- **Monthly Adventures:** 1-2 day experiences that reset your perspective.
- **Life List:** Long-range dreams that deserve planning, not just wishing.

Fill them in over time. These aren't goals to chase. They're coordinates for living. Use them to guide your weeks and months, not to check boxes, but to **expand your life.**

SECTION A → Daily Moments [5-30 minutes]

List small, repeatable moments that lift your day.
No order. No filter. Just list whatever comes to mind. Even if it feels unrealistic.

→

→

→

→

→

→

→

→

→

→

→

→

→

→

→

→

SECTION B → Monthly Adventures

List 1-2 day adventures that energize your month.
No order. No filter. Just list whatever comes to mind. Even if it feels unrealistic.

→

→

→

→

→

→

→

→

→

→

→

→

→

→

→

→

SECTION C → Life List [long-range dreams]

List the long-range dreams worth building, not just imagining.
No order. No filter. Just list whatever comes to mind. Even if it feels unrealistic.

→

→

→

→

→

→

→

→

→

→

→

→

→

→

→

FILE COPY

Quantum Leap Jumpstart

The "Last Year" Test: If this was your final year on Earth, how would you spend your Life-Hours? What would matter more? One more gadget or one more hike with your kids? A closet refresh or a long dinner with friends? A new purse or a ticket to a city you've never seen?

You don't need a diagnosis to live like your time is **precious.** You just need to **decide** to treat it that way.

Let Go, Lean In

Decluttering clears space. Experiences bring life into it.
Now go build a life that feels rich, not just full of stuff.

Building Experience Rituals and Memory Banks

You really don't need a passport or a bucket list to live a life rich in experience. You need **rhythm**, **ritual**, and **repetition with intention.**

Let's build a system for collecting memories the way some people collect stamps, only you're curating **joy, depth, and self-respect.**

OUR LIVES ARE NOT MEASURED BY THE NUMBER OF DAYS, BUT BY THE DENSITY OF MOMENTS.

Create Experience Rituals

Think small and intentional.

Here are examples of small rituals you can build into your life:

- Tuesday morning walk before the world wakes up
- Sunday night phone call with your best friend
- Monthly museum visit or bookstore adventure
- First coffee outdoors each day, no phone allowed
- Celebratory solo dinner when you finish a big task

These are more than habits. They're identity markers. Rituals remind you who you are. They protect your time from the trivial.

Put Pen to Paper: Build Your Experience Blueprint

Day/Time	Ritual Description	Emotional Payoff

Build a Memory Bank

You've heard of a gratitude journal. This goes **deeper.**

Start a Memory Bank, a simple notebook or digital file where you capture:

- A new place you explored
- A moment that made you laugh
- A time you felt fully present
- Something you completed on your own

Return to it when you feel stuck. Let your own memories remind you who you're becoming.

Deposit a Memory

- **Name one recent moment that reminded you you're alive.**

→

- **Why did it matter?**

→

- **How can you create something like it again?**

→

Objects depreciate. **Memories compound.**
There's science behind that.

The Myth of Productivity and the Power of Presence

We've been sold a toxic myth: that productivity is the highest virtue. That your value is measured by how much you produce. That if you're not working, improving, or optimizing, you're wasting time.

Let's call it what it is: productivity worship. You're not a machine. **You're a moment-to-moment miracle.**

The truth? Presence outperforms productivity in every meaningful way.

Productivity Feels Like...

- Achievement without satisfaction
- Always needing to do more
- Guilt during rest
- Feeling behind, even when you're ahead

Presence Feels Like...

- Noticing the wind on your face.
- Tasting your food, every bite.
- Listening without waiting to speak.
- Being fully here, not ahead or behind.

Presence is where life actually happens.

YOUR ATTENTION IS YOUR MOST SACRED ASSET. SPEND IT WHERE YOU FEEL FULLY ALIVE.

Put Pen to Paper:
Your Presence Inventory

When was the last time you:

- **Ate a meal without multitasking?**

→

- **Watched a sunset without photographing it?**

→

- **Had a conversation without checking your phone?**

→

- **Did absolutely nothing and felt peace instead of panic?**

→

The Time-Worth Test

When choosing how to spend your Life-Hours, ask:

- Will this make me feel more alive?
- Will I remember this in five years?
- Am I doing this because it matters, or because I'm afraid to be still?

If **presence** isn't built into your schedule, productivity will own it.

Quantum Leap Jumpstart

- **Name one productivity obsession you can release.**
    - **Obsession: →**

- **Choose a replacement that brings you peace.**
    - **Peace Practice: →**

The Power of Shared Experiences

Some of the best moments in life don't just happen to us; they happen with others.

Shared experiences are emotional amplifiers. They magnify joy, soften struggle, and deepen our connection to life, and each other.

They turn an average event into a lifelong memory. They make us feel seen, supported, and real.
And yet, in a world obsessed with productivity and personal branding, shared presence is increasingly rare.

We text instead of talk. We watch instead of participate. We scroll instead of sit face-to-face.

Let's reclaim the power of shared life.

LIFE IS NOT A SOLO PERFORMANCE. IT'S A JAM SESSION.

Why Shared Experiences Matter

Shared Experience	What It Builds
family meal	belonging, consistency
camping with friends	adventure, bonding, storytelling
group challenge (race, hike)	collective growth, confidence
volunteering with others	meaning, contribution
attending a live event	presence, culture, awe

Put Pen to Paper: Relationship Energy Audit

Think of three people you care about.

Ask yourself:

- When was the last time we shared something real?
- How do I usually show up with them, present or distracted?
- What's one experience we could plan together?

Person	Last Shared Experience	Feeling It Created	New Idea to Share Next

INTIMACY DOESN'T JUST HAPPEN:
IT'S DESIGNED. WITH TIME, ENERGY, AND INTENTION.

Quantum Leap Jumpstart

Consider this quietly:
What if you scheduled a monthly experience with each of your top three people, no gifts, no obligations, just presence?

What would shift in your relationships, your identity, or your memory bank?

The Cost of Numb Living vs. Fully Engaged Living

Let's name it: most people are not living, they're managing. Floating. Scrolling. Reacting.

We're not short on time, we're short on presence. Because we've trained ourselves to avoid discomfort by checking out.

And numb living has a **cost.**
It robs you of wonder. It steals your energy. It dulls your instincts. It disconnects you from people you love.

Being "fine" is often the enemy of being **fully alive.**

Signs You Might Be Numbing

- You default to your phone the second there's silence
- You binge shows and feel more empty after than before
- You shop for things you don't need to feel something
- You say *"I'm tired"* but mean *"I'm uninspired"*

We were not built to coast.
You were designed to **experience**, not escape.

Fully Engaged Living Looks Like...

- Taking walks without headphones
- Asking better questions at dinner
- Noticing the colors of a street you walk every day
- Cooking something slowly and with love
- Saying "*yes*" to spontaneous invitations

It's about letting life actually touch you again. Even the hard parts. **Especially the hard parts.**

Numbing vs. Nourishing Inventory

Daily Habit	Is This Numbing?	Is This Nourishing?
late-night scrolling	☐	☐
binge-watching alone	☐	☐
mindful tea ritual	☐	☐
talking to a close friend	☐	☐
hourly inbox checks	☐	☐

- **Now replace one numbing habit with a nourishing one this week:**
  - **Replace: →**
  - **With: →**

Discomfort is not the enemy. Numbness is.
Let your Life-Hours be **felt**, not avoided.

YOU HAVE TO WAKE UP.
YOU'RE LOSING DAYS YOU'LL NEVER GET BACK.

The Experience Legacy

At the end of your life, no one will talk about how clean your baseboards were. Or how organized your junk drawer was. Or how perfectly you curated your closet.
They'll talk about how you made them feel. What you made together. The moments that couldn't be bought.
That's your Experience Legacy.

People remember presence, not possessions.
This isn't about being dramatic. It's about being honest.

We all leave behind echoes. Some are shelves full of forgotten trinkets. Others are belly laughs, road trips, hard conversations, dancing barefoot in the kitchen.

Now ask: Which one are you building?

- **Quick Reflection:**

Put Pen to Paper:

The Experience Eulogy

- **Imagine someone you love is giving your eulogy:**
  - What do you want them to say?
  - What stories do you want told?
  - What shared experiences do you hope they remember?
  - What kind of energy did you bring to their life?

Write it. →

Now ask: Are you living that legacy?
If not, start **today.**

Don't wait to be remembered for what you owned. Be remembered for how **fully** you lived.

Quantum Leap Jumpstart

Choose one memory you want to build with intention. Make it real.

- **The memory:**

→

- **The person**

→

- **When it happens:**

→

Get on it. Make it real.
Because in the end, the moments you create are the ones that carry **forward**.

- **Field Log [D4] Reflections:**

REALITY CHECK: CHRONOS

INFINITE SCROLL, FINITE BRAIN

FIELD LOG	SECTOR E5	SEQ: [05/11]

INFINITE SCROLL, FINITE BRAIN

You've felt that twitch to check your phone.
The casual scroll that turns into an hour.
Tabs multiplying like rabbits.

We are flooded with information and left hungry for meaning. Our brains, built for survival in a world of scarcity, are now suffocating in a world of surplus.
Noise. Never-ending feeds.

This chapter is about reclaiming your mental bandwidth. It means realizing that just because something is available doesn't mean it deserves your attention. It means resisting the pull of the infinite scroll and choosing what truly feeds your **mind**, your **soul**, your **life**.

The Attention Economy Is Real

You're not just using apps, they're using you. Every second you spend on a screen is tracked, analyzed, optimized to sell you more. Your attention is worth real money. Entire teams of behavioral scientists, UI/UX engineers, and algorithms are working to keep your eyes glued, your thumb scrolling, your dopamine loop cycling.

When you don't pay with money, you pay with **attention**.

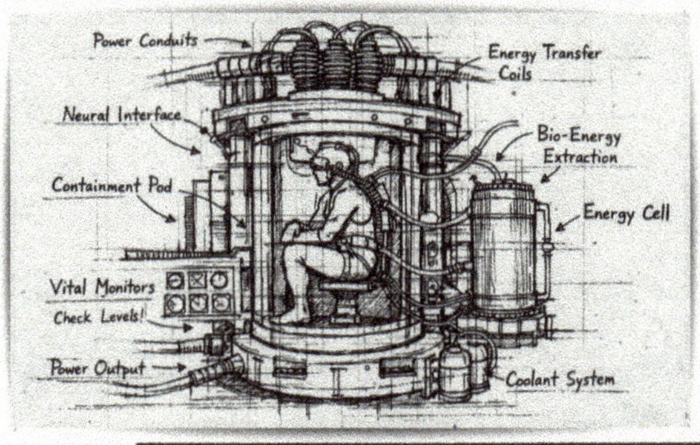

Let’s name what’s happening

- Autoplay traps
- Notifications as dopamine bait
- Endless feeds that scroll forever so you keep going.
- FOMO-engineered marketing (Fear of Missing Out)
- Reward systems that mimic slot machines

Every “like” is a lever. Every click is a contract. And your brain? It’s **overwhelmed. Fragmented. Fried.**

Mental Bandwidth and Decision Fatigue

- When everything competes for your attention, nothing gets it.
- We make tens of thousands of decisions per day. The more inputs you consume, the more decisions you're forced to make, consciously or not.
- All of it is energy. All of it drains your mental reserves.

Attention is a currency. **Spend it where your values live.**

Mental Bandwidth and Decision Fatigue

- When everything competes for your attention, nothing gets it.
- We make tens of thousands of decisions per day. The more inputs you consume, the more decisions you're forced to make, consciously or not.
- All of it is energy. All of it drains your mental reserves.

Attention is a currency. **Spend it where your values live.**

The Brain Bandwidth Audit

- **Estimate your daily screen time:**
  - **Phone: →**
  - **Computer: →**
  - **TV: →**
- **List the top 3 apps or platforms you spend the most time on:**

1.

2.

3.

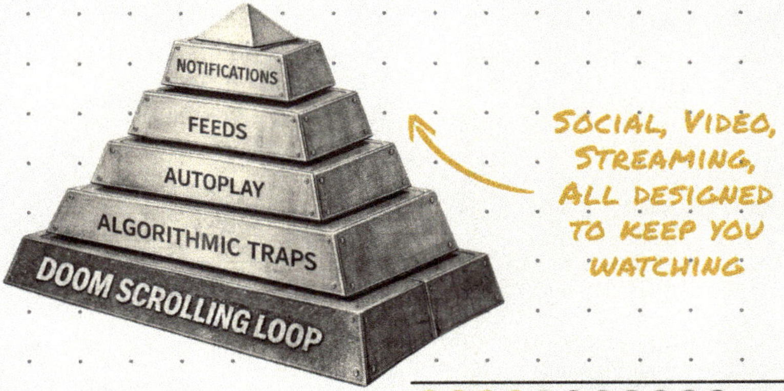

Now ask: What's the emotional result after an hour on each?

Platform	Time/Day	Emotion After Use	Useful or Draining?
			☐ U ☐ D
			☐ U ☐ D
			☐ U ☐ D
			☐ U ☐ D
			☐ U ☐ D
			☐ U ☐ D

- **What could you replace just 30 minutes of scrolling with each day?**

☐ A walk outside
☐ Meditation
☐ Reading a physical book
☐ Journaling
☐ Calling someone you love
☐ Other:

The Myth of Multitasking

Spoiler: multitasking is mostly a lie.

You're not doing multiple things at once, you're switching between them, and every switch carries a cognitive cost.

Attention doesn't teleport. It lingers.

Move when the moment closes, not when distraction pulls you away.

Focus is your secret weapon. **Presence is your superpower.**

THE HUNTER WHO PURSUES TWO RABBITS ENDS UP WITH NONE.

Multitasking is Not Speed but Erosion

Multitasking looks efficient from the outside, but inside your head it often feels messy. Each switch leaves something behind, a fragment of the last task still running while the next one is already asking for space. By the middle of the day your attention can be stretched across half-finished moments, and none of them ever fully close.

That background noise adds up, not as drama but as friction. You reread the same sentence. You walk into a room and forget why. Simple decisions take longer than they should, not because you're incapable, but because your bandwidth is crowded.

The brain settles when it can stay with something long enough to understand it and move it forward. Completion has a physical effect. Your shoulders drop. The pressure eases. Energy returns because nothing unfinished is chasing you anymore.

Momentum grows from that steadiness. One completed action creates room for the next. Attention stacks instead of splintering, and the day stops feeling like a scramble.

Stay with a task until it reaches a natural pause and let it end cleanly, then move. That's where **clarity** starts to return.

Philosophers on Divided Attention

W. James (1842-1910, United States)
Attention defines experience. A divided mind lives a divided life.
He argued that attention is the mechanism that creates reality itself.
Split attention means split experience. A scattered mind doesn't just perform worse, it lives worse. Multitasking, in James's frame, is a tax on reality.

FIG. 1. W. JAMES

Split attention means split experience. A scattered mind doesn't just perform worse, it lives worse. Multitasking, in James's frame, is a tax on reality.

S. Weil (1909–1943, France)
Full attention is respect. Fragmented attention refuses reality.
To her, giving attention was an act of reverence toward the world. When attention fragments, existence becomes shallow. Multitasking is not efficiency. It is a refusal to meet reality fully.

FIG. 2. S. WEIL

B. Pascal (1623–1662, France)
Human misery begins when we cannot sit quietly alone.
He warned that restlessness is not harmless. The inability to remain still drives people toward distraction, noise, and endless diversion. Multitasking is the modern expression of that same urge to fill every quiet moment.

FIG. 3. B. PASCAL

M. Heidegger (1889–1976, Germany)
Constant distraction is escape disguised as activity.
He saw scattered attention as anesthesia. Busyness becomes a shield against meaning. In that state, motion replaces direction. Multitasking is not productivity. It is avoidance dressed as action.

FIG. 4. M. HEIDEGGER

H. Arendt (1906–1975, Germany)
Thought needs pauses. Without silence, experience never becomes understanding.
She believed thinking happens in the gaps, when action stops and reflection begins. A mind that never settles never digests what it lives through. Multitasking erases the space where understanding forms.

FIG. 5. H. ARENDT

F. Nietzsche (1844-1900, Germany)
Depth requires exclusion. Focus grows where distraction is denied.
He believed great work demanded ruthless protection of attention. Without exclusion you become reactive instead of creative. Depth needs continuity. Multitasking destroys continuity.

FIG. 6. F.NIETESGHE

Quantum Leap Jumpstart

What would happen if you turned off all non-essential notifications for 7 days?
What might you notice, feel, reclaim?

- ☐ **Start Date:**

- ☐ **End Date:**

Digital Fasting: The Cleanse You Actually Need

Forget juice cleanses. Your mind needs a digital detox more than your body needs celery juice. Digital fasting means setting **intentional boundaries** on your tech use, short or long, so your nervous system can reset, your creativity can breathe, and your brain can stop spinning like a browser with 37 open tabs.

Types of Digital Fasts:

Fast Type	Duration	Purpose
screen-free mornings	1-2 hours daily	protect clarity and presence
24-hour digital sabbath	once a week	reclaim stillness and reset
app fasts (single app)	7+ days	break habit, assess need
notification fast	ongoing	end reaction-based behavior

Quantum Leap Jumpstart

The 7-Day Mental Reset:

What would happen if you turned off all non-essential notifications for 7 days? What might you notice, feel, reclaim?

☐ Remove one distracting app as an experiment.

- **App Name:** →

☐ Journal how you feel at the end of each day.

Day	Notes on Mood/Clarity/Presence
1	
2	
3	
4	
5	
6	
7	

Did your anxiety drop? Did your creativity rise? What did you notice?

Now ask: Do I want that app back at all?

YOU DON'T NEED MORE CONTENT.

YOU NEED MORE CONSCIOUSNESS.

The Curation Mindset

Choose Your Inputs Like You Choose Your Friends:
Curation is the antidote to overwhelm.
Your brain isn't a landfill. It's a living garden. Everything you allow in, every article, post, book, video, podcast, is a seed.

The question is: do you like what's growing?
Let's stop hoarding information like we're going to be quizzed in the afterlife. The internet is infinite. **Your time is not.**

Key Principle

The fact that you only have so many Life-Hours left is what makes your attention **sacred**. So treat it like your home. Don't let just anything inside.

Start thinking like a museum curator:

- Not everything belongs in your gallery.
- Just because it's interesting doesn't mean it's essential.
- Fewer, better inputs = clearer thinking + more original output.

Put Pen to Paper:

Your Input Filter

- **Audit five sources you currently consume, then audit their worth:**

Source/Platform	Does It Bring Value?	Distraction or Nourishment?	Keep / Reduce / Delete
	□ Y □ N	□ D □ N	□ K □ R □ D
	□ Y □ N	□ D □ N	□ K □ R □ D
	□ Y □ N	□ D □ N	□ K □ R □ D
	□ Y □ N	□ D □ N	□ K □ R □ D
	□ Y □ N	□ D □ N	□ K □ R □ D

Now ask: What 3 new high-quality sources could you explore instead?

1.
2.
3.

- **Quick Reflection:**

YOU DON'T NEED MORE INPUT. YOU NEED STRICTER FILTERS.

Curation Tips for a Sharper Mind

- Create a "Park It Here" list so curiosity doesn't hijack your day. Write it down. Don't chase it now.
- Cut anything you follow out of habit, not intention. If it doesn't earn attention, it doesn't stay.
- Give the News a schedule instead of letting it barge in. You visit it. It doesn't visit you.
- Reserve one window each week for long-form ideas. Depth needs protected time.

"Priorities," like "multitasking," are myths, modern illusions. We can only focus on one thing at a time. Make sure it's what matters most.

Shape your feed around it, not around whatever is designed to pull you away.
Your attention isn't a storage closet. It's a workbench. You need room to work.

Clear it. Protect it. Use it on purpose.

- **Quick Reflection:**

YOU BECOME WHAT YOU CONSUME.
FILTER ACCORDINGLY.

The Cost of Overconsumption

Call it what it is: a slow leak in your capacity to think clearly.
Overconsumption isn't about quantity, it's about collision.
Too many inputs fighting for the same inch of mental space. Too much noise, not enough recovery.
Overconsumption scrambles your thinking and dulls your instincts.

Your mind can't integrate when it's flooded.
It can't create when it's reacting.
It can't rest when it's crowded.

Signs you're overloaded:

- You reach for your phone before you know why
- You take in more than you can recall
- Your attention jumps without your permission
- Your inner voice sounds like borrowed thoughts
- You can't remember the last thing you finished

More input doesn't sharpen you. It just breaks you into pieces.

- **Quick Reflection:**

Why It's a Problem

- Floods your attention
- Weakens your ability to think clearly
- Blurs emotion instead of helping you feel
- Breaks your capacity to stay present

Consuming = Taking In

You are the audience:

- Scrolling social media
- Watching streaming platforms
- Reading news you won't remember
- Listening to endless commentary
- Shopping as distraction
- Collecting advice you never apply

Creating = Putting Out

You're the builder:

- Writing your own pages instead of consuming everyone else's
- Making art, design, or something with your hands
- Recording your thoughts, ideas, or stories
- Starting a project instead of thinking about one
- Cooking something real instead of ordering convenience
- Building, crafting, shaping something that exists because you choose to act

Processing = Integrating

You're digesting what you've taken in:

- Journaling what mattered
- Summarizing the ideas you want to keep
- Mapping or sketching the next move
- Having conversations that sharpen you
- Reflecting in silence
- Turning insight into decisions
- Organizing what you know into something usable

The Input-to-Output Ratio

Activity Type	Current Hours/Week	Notes
consuming		
creating		
processing		

Turning insight into action:

- **I will limit consuming:** ______ hours per day.
- **I will be creating:** ______ hours per day, ______ times per week.
- **I will be processing:** ______ hours per day.

Every swipe has the psychology of a slot machine, delivering random rewards. That single mechanic is enough to capture your focus for hours.

YOUR FOCUS COLLAPSES WHEN YOU LET EVERYTHING IN. CHOOSE WHAT EARNS YOUR ATTENTION.

The Input-to-Output Ratio

Activity Type	Mode	Impact
consuming	passive intake	feeds distraction or growth
creating	active output	raises energy, fulfillment
processing	mental digestion	feeds wisdom, clarity

Most people consume endlessly without creating or processing. Over time, it turns into overwhelm, anxiety, and the quiet feeling of being stuck.

- **Quick Reflection:**

INPUT IS FINE.
JUST DON'T LET IT REPLACE YOUR OWN THINKING.

Build a New Brain Diet: Feed Your Mind What It Deserves

We know this about food: what you take in shapes how you feel. Your mind works the same way. So let's build a mental diet that actually supports the life you want.

Step 1: Clear the Mental Clutter

- **Clear Out:**
  - Manipulative influencers
  - Outrage-driven headlines
  - Anxiety-loop news cycles
  - Passive how-to rabbit holes
  - Mindless meme dumps

Now ask: Does this input sharpen my mind, or drain my energy?

Step 2: Rebuild Your Input List

Mental Fuel	Example Sources	Effect
deep insight	books, long-form ideas	strengthens perspective
emotional truth	essays, documentaries	deepens understanding
quiet space	nature, journaling	restores clarity
strategic input	biographies, frameworks	builds capability
creative spark	art, music, theater	ignites imagination

BUILD A BRAIN YOU'RE PROUD TO THINK WITH.

Put Pen to Paper:
Build Your Brain Plate

Brain Meal Time	Current Input	Better Nourishment
morning		
midday		
evening		
before bed		

What you consume becomes your content. Your tone. **Your life lens.**

The Noise Detox

Turning Down the Volume on Everything That Doesn't Feed Your Peace

If your brain were a room, right now it would probably be cluttered, loud, and flashing with blinking neon signs. We need to clear the space. Dim the lights. Lower the volume.
Noise isn't just sound. It's mental clutter. It's anything that takes up attention without giving clarity in return. And modern life is full of it.

Types of Noise:

- Background TV
- Email alerts every 3 minutes
- Ads at every scroll and corner
- Useless comparisons from social media
- Opinions you didn't ask for
- Your own critical inner monologue

SPEAK TO A FRIEND THE WAY YOU SPEAK TO YOURSELF, AND WATCH THEM WALK AWAY.

Noise Has a Cost:

- It reduces your ability to hear your own thoughts
- It blocks creative ideas from surfacing
- It drowns out emotional cues from your body
- It builds anxiety without useful action

YOU CAN'T HEAR YOUR LIFE CALLING IF EVERYTHING IS SCREAMING.

Detox Steps

I. **Audit Your Inputs:**
   - What notifications can be turned off?
   - What background noise do you tolerate daily?
   - What sources do you check "just in case" that never add value?

II. **Design Silence Into Your Day:**
   - Start the day with 10 minutes of quiet before screens
   - Eat at least one meal without media
   - Create "no-input zones" (walks, restrooms and waiting rooms)

III. **Remove Digital Background Clutter:**
   - Declutter your desktop
   - Reduce visual chaos (tabs, widgets and toolbars)
   - Turn off autoplay features

IV. **Quiet the Inner Critic:**
   - Practice stillness
   - Replace self-judgment with simple noticing
   - Name the noise. Then release it

YOU DON'T NEED MORE TIME.
YOU NEED MORE SILENCE IN THE TIME YOU ALREADY HAVE.

- **Quick Reflection:**

Put Pen to Paper:

Noise Audit

Where does noise creep into your day? What does it keep you from noticing?

Time of Day	Common Noise	Emotion It Causes	One Change I Could Make
morning			
midday			
evening			

- **What is your new rule for what gets to enter your mind?**

→

CREATE A LIFE WHERE YOUR PEACE IS LOUDER THAN THE NOISE.

- **Field Log [E5] Reflections:**

REALITY CHECK: CHRONOS

EVERY MEAL COUNTS

FIELD LOG | SECTOR F6 | SEQ: [06/11]

EVERY MEAL COUNTS

Food isn't just fuel. It's culture. It's memory. It's time.

You'll eat thousands more meals in your lifetime, if you're lucky.

But here's the truth: most of them pass by unnoticed. Rushed. Scrolled through. Forgotten.

This chapter is about reclaiming those moments. It's about honoring the sacredness of nourishment. And it's about facing the absurd waste we've normalized in a culture addicted with convenience.

Let's reset the plate.

The Numbers You Can't Ignore

Let's do the math.
If you eat lunch and dinner from age 2 to 100, you will have about 35,770 lunches and 35,770 dinners,
for a total of 71,540 real meal chances.

Now ask: How many of those meals will you actually remember?

→

Every lunch and dinner is a ticket, a chance to nourish yourself, to connect, to slow time. Or to waste it.

Choose well.

The Hidden Cost of Convenience

We say we're too busy to cook. So we buy plastic-wrapped calories. We over-purchase, under-plan, toss out leftovers, and microwave things in containers we know aren't safe.

It's killing more than our nutrition. **It's killing our connection.** To our bodies. To the people we eat with. To the planet.

Waste Stats to Swallow:

- Roughly 30–40% of food in the U.S. is wasted
- Over 130 billion pounds of food every year
- Most of it is grown, packaged, transported, and bought... then trashed
- Landfills are full of food waste emitting methane, a potent greenhouse gas

And here's the kicker: you paid for that food with Life-Hours.
You traded your working time for something you never ate.

Put Pen to Paper:

The Meal Audit

Think about your last 7 days:

Meal Time	Eaten Mindfully?	Was it Nourishing?	Waste Created?
breakfast	☐ YES ☐ NO	☐ YES ☐ NO	☐ YES ☐ NO
lunch	☐ YES ☐ NO	☐ YES ☐ NO	☐ YES ☐ NO
dinner	☐ YES ☐ NO	☐ YES ☐ NO	☐ YES ☐ NO

During that week, how many meals were:

- Rushed? →
+ Meals truly savored? →
- In front of a screen? →
- Forgotten before bedtime? →

- Mindless? →
+ Cooked? →
+ Shared? →
- Skipped? →

What would it mean to reclaim one meal a day as sacred?

Emotional Eating vs. Intentional Nourishment

Food is emotional. Always has been. From birthday cakes to pints of heartbreak ice cream, we eat feelings more often than we admit.
And that's okay... sometimes. But when food becomes the main emotional outlet, it's time for a **reset.**

Emotional Eating Red Flags:

- Eating when you're not hungry
- Craving specific textures (crunchy = anger, creamy = comfort)
- Guilt after meals
- Mindless snacking while stressed, bored, or sad

Intentional nourishment means eating to feel **alive**, not just less **empty**.

It means asking: What do I need? Energy? Grounding? Connection?

Eating to avoid feeling is like trying to silence a fire alarm by pulling the batteries.

Instead, ask what the **emotion** is asking you to feed.

*EAT LIKE SOMEONE WHO RESPECTS TIME:
FUEL YOURSELF LIKE YOUR HOURS MATTER.*

Put Pen to Paper:
Emotional Eating Tracker

For the next 3 meals, **pause** before you eat.

Meal	Am I Hungry?	Emotion Present	Did I Choose with Intention?
1.	☐ YES ☐ NO		☐ YES ☐ NO
2.	☐ YES ☐ NO		☐ YES ☐ NO
3.	☐ YES ☐ NO		☐ YES ☐ NO

The Art of Shared Meals

A meal shared is a moment **multiplied**.

Eating together has always been more than survival. It's community. Ritual. Celebration. Medicine. From family dinners and coffee with a friend to breaking bread with strangers, sharing food is one of the oldest ways we say - ***"You matter. I see you. Let's pause together."***

But in today's rush-and-scroll world, shared meals are becoming endangered. We eat in cars. At desks. Alone. On autopilot.

It's time to bring the table back.

IN A WORLD OF NOISE, THE RIGHT MEAL FEELS LIKE COMING HOME.

Why Shared Meals Matter

- **They deepen connection:** Eye contact. Laughter. Conversation. Silence. These moments bond us.
- **They improve health:** People who eat together regularly tend to have better nutrition and lower stress levels.
- **They teach presence:** Sharing space requires slowing down. Listening. Noticing.
- **They mark time:** Meals become milestones. Stories. Anchors in memory.

We don't just remember the food. **We remember who we were with.**

Put Pen to Paper: Shared Meal Inventory

In the past month:

- **How many meals did you eat with someone else?**

→

- **How many felt present, connected, unrushed?**

→

- **Who do you miss sharing meals with?**

→

SHARING A MEAL IS HOW WE CELEBRATE LIFE, LAUGHTER, AND THE SIMPLE JOY OF BEING TOGETHER.

Now:

- **Who will you invite to your next meal?**

→

- **What kind of moment do you want to create?**

→

- **Who do you miss sharing meals with?**

→

SOME MEALS FEED THE BODY. THE BEST ONES FEED THE SOUL: SHARED, SAVORED, AND REMEMBERED.

A shared meal isn't just a plate. **It's a presence practice.**

Mindful Eating Rituals

The Lost Art of Presence at the Plate:
When you slow down at the table, you speed up your healing.
Mindful eating isn't about rules or diets. It's about attention. It's about giving the act of nourishment the space and reverence it deserves.
One meal. One bite. Fully **present**.

Create Your Ritual

Rituals create rhythm. Rhythm creates peace.

Here are ways to infuse intentionality into every meal:

- **The Pause:**
  - Sit. Breathe. Notice the food in front of you.
  - **Ask yourself:** Where did this come from? What had to happen for this meal to exist?

- **The Gratitude Anchor:**
  - Say thank you. Out loud or in silence. To the earth. The grower. The cook. Yourself.
- **The No-Device Zone:**
  - Meals are sacred. Phones go away.
  - Replace screen time with human connection or silence.
- **The Slower Pace:**
  - Chew. Rest between bites. Savor textures, spices, aromas.
- **The Closing Breath:**
  - When the meal ends, don't just stand up. Breathe. Notice how you feel.
  - **Acknowledge:** That was nourishment. I honored it.

WHAT YOU EAT SHAPES YOUR BODY.
HOW YOU EAT SHAPES YOUR RELATIONSHIP WITH FOOD.

Put Pen to Paper:

Your Meal Ritual Builder

- **My Meal Start Ritual:**

→

- **Mealtime Rules:**
  (e.g., no screens, music only, light a candle)

→

- **My Closing Practice:**

→

- **What does eating with intention give you that rushing never could?**

→

YOU ARE THE HEAD CHEF OF YOUR LIFE,
NO PLATE LEAVES YOUR KITCHEN WITHOUT YOUR FINAL SAY.

QUALITY, INTENTION, AND PRIDE IN EVERY DETAIL
ARE THE STANDARD, NOT THE EXCEPTION.

A Global Lens:

Not Everyone Eats the Same Way

When we gather around a table, we might assume mealtime rituals are universal, but across the world, food and fellowship take wildly different forms.

From the boisterous family feasts of Italy to the quiet, reverent meals of Japan, every culture brings its own rhythm, rules, and meaning to sharing food.

Understanding these traditions reminds us that connection isn't about doing things the same way; it's about honoring the moment, the people, and the spirit behind it.

In Italy:

- Meals are celebrations of life.
  Eating together is sacred; loud conversations, laughter, and many courses are the norm.
  No one rushes. Meals can last for hours.

In China:

- Meals are deeply communal.
  Dishes are placed in the center and shared; individual plates are rare.
  Respect for elders at the table is a key custom.

In Turkey:

- Hospitality is a point of pride; you never leave a Turkish table hungry.
  Meals are lively, generous, and center around sharing *meze* (small dishes).
  Guests are treated like royalty.

In Mexico:

- Food equals family.
  Eating together is the heart of gatherings, from tiny street taco stands to giant family feasts.
  Meals are loud, warm, and often involve storytelling and music.

In Japan:

- Meals are quiet, respectful, and focused.
  It's polite to say "itadakimasu" before eating (I receive this meal with gratitude) and "gochisousama deshita" after (thank you for the feast/meal). Appreciation of the food and those who prepared it is central.

In Ethiopia:

- Meals are eaten from a shared platter with hands.
  Gursha (feeding someone else) is a gesture of deep care.
  Sharing food is an act of love and community.

In France:

- Meals are social events; slow, elegant, and layered with conversation.
  Courses flow naturally, and savoring every bite is an unwritten rule.
  Dining is about connection, not just food.

In India:

- Meals are highly communal and spiritual.
  Sharing food strengthens bonds; food is seen as a blessing.
  Eating with hands is traditional, connecting more intimately with the meal.

What's the common thread? These cultures may differ wildly in how they gather, but **they share one unbreakable truth**: Meals are never just about food; they are about **connection**.

Whether loud or quiet, formal or casual, every tradition protects something sacred, the act of pausing, sharing, and strengthening the bonds that hold people together.

Redefining Indulgence: Pleasure Without Regret

We've been sold a lie: that indulgence means excess.
More food. More sugar. More wine. More spending.
More *"treat yourself"* culture.

But real indulgence, the kind that nourishes rather than numbs, is something else entirely.
It's presence. It's depth. It's choosing quality over quantity.

True indulgence doesn't leave you heavy; it leaves you lit up.

- **What Indulgence Isn't:**
  - Guilt-laced binges
  - Consumption to escape
  - Mindless overdoing it
  - Spending energy or money you don't have
- **What Indulgence Can Be:**
  - A single, perfect square of dark chocolate enjoyed slowly
  - A homemade meal shared with a loved one
  - A walk outside with nothing in your ears but the wind
  - Time blocked out to do absolutely nothing

Real indulgence doesn't require excess. It requires **intention.**

Put Pen to Paper:

Indulgence Inventory

- What have you been calling *"indulgence"* that actually drains you?

→

- What are 3 ways you could indulge with awareness?

1.
2.
3.

- What's the most luxurious thing you can do for your soul this week?

→

YOU DON'T NEED MORE STUFF, YOU NEED MORE MEANING.

Leftovers, Gratitude, and the Full Circle

Reclaiming Food as Story, Not Just Fuel.

Leftovers get a bad rap. But they're not second-class meals; they're memory keepers. They're proof that something was prepared with care. That you had enough. That your table was full.

Food, like life, is better when it's used **completely.**

We often treat meals as moments to consume, not to remember. But every dish holds a story. A lineage. A moment worth honoring.

- **What Leftovers Teach Us:**
  - **Gratitude:** This meal didn't appear by magic. It came from sun, soil, hands, and time.
  - **Mindfulness:** Leftovers slow us down. They invite us to pause. Reflect.
  - **Resourcefulness:** Using everything you have is an act of wisdom, not lack.

Wasting food is wasting life. Reusing it is respecting it.

Put Pen to Paper: Gratitude Loop

Think of the last meal you enjoyed:

- Who grew it?
- Who transported it?
- Who prepared it?
- What emotion or memory does it bring up?

Now ask:

- What would it mean to eat the same food again, with more presence?

→

GRATITUDE IS FUEL.
AND MOST PEOPLE FORGET
TO FILL THE TANK.

- What could you do with the scraps?
  (broth, compost, dog treats?)

→

- What leftover habits do you want to keep for life?

→

NOTHING IS "LEFT OVER" WHEN YOU'RE PAYING ATTENTION.

The Full Circle Ritual

- **Reclaim the cycle of respect:**
    - Plan meals with purpose.
    - Cook with intention.
    - Eat with presence.
    - Respect your leftovers; save them with care.
    - Repurpose what remains.

Saving is not about scarcity.
It's about honoring the effort behind every ingredient, every hand that touched it, every moment shared around the table.
It's about stewardship, gratitude, and wisdom, not lack.

When we close the loop with care, we live with a deeper kind of **abundance**.

- **Quick Reflection:**

A MEAL ISN'T OVER WHEN CHEWING STOPS.
IT ENDS WHEN GRATITUDE IS FELT
AND THE LEFTOVERS ARE HONORED.

- **Field Log [F6] Reflections:**

REALITY CHECK: CHRONOS

YOUR SOCIAL TIME BUDGET

FIELD LOG	SECTOR G7	SEQ: [07/11]

YOUR SOCIAL TIME BUDGET

Time is currency. And relationships are one of the most expensive and most rewarding ways we spend it.

But here's the hard truth: You don't have time for everyone. You barely have enough time for the people who truly matter.

This chapter is about auditing your social life, not to be cold or calculated, but to finally be intentional. To stop saying yes out of guilt. To stop giving your best hours to people who leave you drained, and to start investing where it really counts.

The Human Ledger

Think of your time like a social bank account. Every interaction is either a deposit or a withdrawal. Some leave you energized, understood, seen. Others leave you doubting yourself, exhausted, or smaller than before.

It's not about being transactional. It's about being **honest.**
You wouldn't leave your financial accounts open to random strangers. So why treat your time any differently?

Time by the Numbers

A quick example: You have roughly 315,616 waking hours left if you're 46 and lucky enough to reach 100. Let's say work, chores, and life admin take up 60% of that (189,370 hours). That leaves about **126,246 hours** for everything else including rest, creativity, and social life.

If you spend 2 hours a day interacting with others:

- That's 730 hours per year
- That's 39,420 hours from now until 100

Now ask: Who gets those hours?
And more importantly, **who deserves them?**

Your Social Audit

List the 10 people you spend the most time with in an average week:

Name	Hours/Week	Energy After
1.		☐ Positive ☐ Negative ☐ Neutral
2.		☐ Positive ☐ Negative ☐ Neutral
3.		☐ Positive ☐ Negative ☐ Neutral
4.		☐ Positive ☐ Negative ☐ Neutral
5.		☐ Positive ☐ Negative ☐ Neutral
6.		☐ Positive ☐ Negative ☐ Neutral
7.		☐ Positive ☐ Negative ☐ Neutral
8.		☐ Positive ☐ Negative ☐ Neutral
9.		☐ Positive ☐ Negative ☐ Neutral
10.		☐ Positive ☐ Negative ☐ Neutral

- **Which of these people:**
  - Challenge you to grow?
  - Encourage your dreams?
  - Respect your time and energy?
  - Drain your focus or consistently offload their drama?

BOUNDARIES AREN'T BARRIERS. THEY'RE FILTERS FOR VALUE.

Understanding Relationship Types

All relationships aren't meant to be lifelong. Some are seasonal. Some are situational. Some are sacred.

- **Let's break it down:**
  - **Lifelines:** People you trust with your truth. Your Inner Circle.
  - **Growth Friends:** Push you. Inspire you. Don't let you coast.
  - **Circle Friends:** You like them. They like you. It's mutual and easy.
  - **Situational:** Coworkers, school friends, proximity-based. Might fade naturally.
  - **Drains:** It's always about them. You leave feeling smaller. It's not healthy.

- **Quick Reflection:**

Time to categorize

You don't have to cut people out, but you do have to decide what you're no longer available for.

Put Pen to Paper:
The Circle Sorter

Name	Category (a–e)	Hours Given This Month	Worth It?
1.			☐ YES ☐ NO
2.			☐ YES ☐ NO
3.			☐ YES ☐ NO
4.			☐ YES ☐ NO
5.			☐ YES ☐ NO

- **What percentage of your social time is going to your top 5 most nourishing relationships?**

☐ 20% or less ☐ 40–60% ☐ 80%+

- **What needs to shift?**

NO ONE SHOULD TREAT YOU LIKE A FREE TRIAL

→

ACCESS TO YOU IS A PRIVILEGE.
NOT EVERYONE DESERVES FRONT-ROW SEATS TO YOUR LIFE.

The Myth of Social Obligation

- **Raise your hand if you've ever:**
    - Gone to an event you didn't want to attend
    - Answered a call you knew would drain you
    - Said yes just to avoid discomfort
    - Stayed in a friendship out of guilt, not joy

Welcome to the myth of social obligation.

We're conditioned to believe that we owe people our time just because we've known them a long time, or they're related to us, or they expect it.
But your time isn't an apology. It's not a subscription. It's a sacred, finite resource.

Just because someone wants access to you doesn't mean they're entitled to it.

Guilt ≠ Obligation

- **Let's break this down:**
    - Guilt is a feeling. Often learned. Often manipulative.
    - Obligation is a choice. Something you intentionally honor.
- **You are allowed to:**
    - Change
    - Grow
    - Outgrow people
    - Set new boundaries
    - Say no without a 20-step explanation

Loving people doesn't mean abandoning yourself.

Put Pen to Paper:

Guilt Map

Person / Group	Why You Feel Obligated?	Is It True or Taught?	Boundary Needed?
1.			☐ YES ☐ NO
2.			☐ YES ☐ NO
3.			☐ YES ☐ NO
4.			☐ YES ☐ NO
5.			☐ YES ☐ NO

- **What's one social obligation you're ready to release this month?**

→

- **What will you do with that freed-up time?**

→

SAYING NO TO WHAT DRAINS YOU IS SAYING YES TO WHO YOU'RE MEANT TO BECOME.

High-Return Relationships: Who Brings Out Your Best?

You've probably heard of high-return investments. You put in effort, and over time, you get way more back.

Some people are exactly like that. They amplify your energy. They expand your thinking. They remind you who you are when you forget. These are your high-return relationships.

- **Signs of a High-Return Relationship:**
    - You leave conversations feeling seen, not judged
    - You laugh. Deep belly laughs. Often.
    - They challenge you to level up without making you feel "less than"
    - You don't have to perform, edit, or filter who you are
    - You feel energized after spending time with them, not drained

Great people don't just fill your time. **They sharpen your edge.**

HERE'S THE TRUTH: YOU DON'T NEED MORE FRIENDS. YOU NEED MORE OF THE RIGHT ONES.

Put Pen to Paper:

Your Top 5 High-Return People

- **List the five people who:**
    - Make you feel most like yourself
    - Support your growth
    - Cheer when you win (and sit quietly with you when you lose)

Name	Why They Matter?	How Can You Invest More?
1.		
2.		
3.		
4.		
5.		

Now Ask: When did you last connect?
Don't wait for the perfect time. Make the damn time.

- **What's one small way you can deepen one of these connections this week?**

- [ ] Call instead of text
- [ ] Send a handwritten note
- [ ] Open up about something real
- [ ] Plan a meal or walk together
- [ ] →
- [ ] →
- [ ] →
- [ ] →
- [ ] →

The Price of Avoiding Loneliness: Why Real Connection Starts Within

Let's be honest: silence scares people.
We reach for our phones in line, scroll in bed, binge-watch through dinner, not because we're curious, but because we're uncomfortable. We're filling space. Filling time. Avoiding loneliness. But loneliness isn't solved by noise. It's only made louder.

The absence of company isn't the problem. It's the absence of **self**.
When you can't sit with yourself, you'll seek the wrong people to distract you. That's how we end up in half-hearted friendships, lukewarm relationships, and overstretched schedules.

Loneliness vs. Aloneness

- Loneliness is disconnection from self.
- Aloneness is the gift of your own presence.
- You don't heal social anxiety by increasing your contact list. You heal it by learning to enjoy your own damn company.

Signs You're Avoiding, Not Connecting

- You text because you're bored, not interested
- You say yes just to have plans
- You feel worse after being with people, not better
- You fear being alone with your thoughts

If you can't recharge alone, you're not choosing relationships, you're hiding in them.

Put Pen to Paper: Silence Inventory

Think back to the last time you spent more than two hours without your phone, no talking, no music, no TV, no podcasts. Just you, in real silence, with no distractions.

- **What showed up when the noise was gone?**

☐ Boredom ☐ Anxiety ☐ Creativity ☐ Peace

LONELINESS FADES THE MOMENT YOU BECOME SOMEONE YOU'RE PROUD TO SIT WITH.

Now ask:

- **What weekly ritual would help me practice being alone with intention?**

→

The Social Budget: Time for What Matters

You don't need a longer to-do list. You need a clearer who-list.
Designing your social time isn't about scheduling hangouts like meetings, it's about aligning your hours with your highest values.
Because when you make time for the right people, the rest of your life feels **lighter. Fuller. Calmer.**

The 3:2:1 Framework

Use this as a weekly rhythm to simplify your social life:

- **3 meaningful touchpoints:** Check in with 3 core people. A call, a text, a coffee, or shared silence

- **2 deeper connections:** Spend focused time with 2 people you want to grow closer to

- **1 vulnerable conversation:** Be real with at least 1 person each week. Go beyond small talk

This isn't rigid. It's a compass.

Make space for who matters,
that's the ultimate relationship ROI.

Social Planning Map

Weekly Rhythm	Person	Plan	Why It Matters?
3 Check-ins	1.		
	2.		
	3.		
2 Deeper Moments	1.		
	2.		
1 Real Conversation	1.		

- **What time of day are you most available to give people your best?**

☐ Morning ☐ Midday ☐ Evening

- **What days are ideal for connection?**

☐ Weekdays ☐ Weekends ☐ Mixed

- **Quick Reflection:**

Quantum Leap Jumpstart

- List the 5 people who get access to the best parts of your time, energy, and presence:

1.
2.
3.
4.
5.

- List the boundaries that keep your relationships strong:

1.
2.
3.
4.
5.

MAKE FEWER PROMISES. KEEP DEEPER ONES.

A Letter to My Inner Circle

This is the group I trust with the real version of me.

Not the highlight reel. Not the polite version. The actual one.

Not everyone gets a seat at this table. This circle is small on purpose. It exists so the people inside it can grow, not shrink. We are here to remind each other who we are when the world gets loud.

If you're in this circle, it means I've chosen you intentionally. You get more access to my time, energy, and attention than most people. That access matters.

Being in this circle isn't about always agreeing or keeping things comfortable. It's about honesty, loyalty, and the ability to call each other out without breaking the friendship. This space is for people who want each other to win, not just socially, but in life.

You will be the person I call when the world gets too heavy. And I will answer your call to support you, listen, and tell you the truth. I will not judge you. I will stand with you.

Here's what I commit to bringing:
I'll be direct instead of passive.
I'll show up when it matters.
I won't disappear when things get messy.
I'll respect your boundaries and expect you to respect mine.

Here's what I need from you:
Choose courage over comfort.
If there's a problem, talk to me directly, not through other people.
Say the hard thing early, not after it explodes.
Don't compete. Lift each other.
Keep trust tight. What's said here stays here.
Protect the friendship by being honest, not polite.

If you sit at this table, **you matter to me.**
Let's protect this circle and make each other stronger inside it.

- **Field Log [G7] Reflections:**

REALITY CHECK: CHRONOS

AD ATTACK!

FIELD LOG	SECTOR H8	SEQ: [08/11]

AD ATTACK!

Let's not sugarcoat it: Your attention is under siege.

Not just your money. Not just your inbox. Your entire consciousness is the new battleground.

Every app, platform, billboard, influencer, and algorithm is designed to hijack your focus and redirect your time toward consumption. Not creation. Not presence. Not connection.

This chapter is your armor. We're going to expose the tactics, rewire your defenses, and reclaim your most precious currency, **your attention.**

Because if you don't choose what to focus on, someone else will, and they're not thinking about your well-being.

The Attention Economy: You're not the customer, you're the product.

Let's be blunt. Most of the tech and media companies that fill your screen time don't make money unless your attention is locked in, and preferably anxious, hungry, or insecure.

They don't want a calm, confident, grounded you. They want a distracted, comparing, triggered version of you.

Why? Because that version clicks more. That version buys more.

How Ads Hack Your Brain

- **Micro-Targeting:** They know what you searched, watched, lingered on, even whispered near your phone
- **Scarcity Triggers:** "Only 3 left." "30% off ends in 2 hours."
- **Social Proof:** "Trending now. 10,000 people bought this."
- **Fear of Missing Out:** Exclusive drops. Timed offers. Limited access.
- **Dopamine Loops:** Scroll. Get a hit. Repeat.

They're not advertising products.
They're selling emotional states.
And renting space in your brain.

Put Pen to Paper: Your Ad Awareness Audit

- **How many ads do you think you saw yesterday?**

→

- Now open your phone or browser history. **What apps or sites did you use the most?**

→

- **Which of those platforms show ads?**

☐ Social media ☐ News ☐ Streaming platforms

☐ Short-form video ☐ Apps & games ☐ Shopping websites

- **How many led to:**
  - A purchase: →
  - A distraction: →
  - A dopamine hit: →

Now Ask: What emotional need did they promise to fulfill?

- **List 3 products/services you've bought in the past 3 months:**

1.
2.
3.

- **What made you buy each one?**

☐ Emotion ☐ Habit ☐ Need ☐ Influence

- **Looking back, which of those purchases actually added value, and which just filled a momentary void?**

→

If the service is free, your attention is the product.

Your Brain on Marketing

Neuroscience confirms: Repeated exposure becomes trust. Even if you don't like a brand, see it enough times and your brain starts choosing it. This is why saturation works. It's not logic, it's low-grade conditioning.
Repetition beats resistance. **Unless you opt out.**

Digital Junk Food: Why We're Overfed and Undernourished

Let's call it what it is: most of what you scroll is processed junk. It's fast. It's addictive. It's engineered to hijack your senses. And it leaves you empty.
If it feels familiar, it's because the average feed is the intellectual equivalent of a gas station hot dog, designed for cravings, not nourishment.

Signs You're Consuming Too Much Digital Junk Food

- You scroll endlessly but can't recall anything meaningful.
- You feel anxious or down after a session.
- You hop from screen to screen without rest.
- You crave content the way others crave sugar.

JUNK CONTENT CREATES JUNK THOUGHTS.

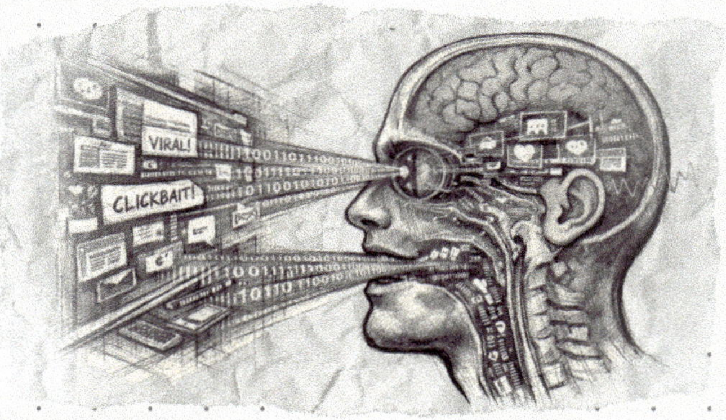

The Dopamine Drain

- Every reel, every swipe, every "ding" is a dopamine drip. But unlike the pleasure of finishing a book or having a deep conversation, this drip has no satisfaction arc. It's novelty without nourishment.
- It creates what psychologists call "attention residue", the scattered fragments of your focus that never return to center.
- A mind full of digital crumbs can't cook a real idea.

Put Pen to Paper:

Content Cleanse Starter Pack

Step 1: What platforms do you spend the most time on?

☐ → ☐ →

☐ → ☐ →

☐ → ☐ →

☐ → ☐ →

Step 2: Time audit. How are you really spending it?

☐ Educational: % ☐ Entertaining: %

☐ Anxiety-producing: % ☐ Mindless filler: %

Step 3: Pick 3 content accounts or creators to unfollow today

1.
2.
3.

Step 4: Replace them with 3 intentional alternatives
(e.g.,longform thinkers, quality artists, calming channels)

1.
2.
3.

The Algorithm Is Not Your Friend: How Hidden Systems Hijack You

Let's kill the fantasy: the algorithm isn't neutral. It's not here to help you grow, heal, or think freely.

It's a code-based puppet master trained on one mission: keep you watching, swiping, clicking, and consuming for as long as humanly possible.
And it does that by studying you. Tracking your behavior.
Learning what holds your gaze and what triggers your nervous system.
Then it feeds you more of it.

IF YOU CAN PROTECT YOUR TIME FROM THEIR ALGORITHM, YOU WIN.

How the Algorithm Rewires Your Mind

- **Engagement Loops:** More of what you react to. Even if you hate it.
- **Emotional Triggers:** Anger, envy, outrage... these keep you scrolling.
- **Confirmation Bias:** It shows you what you already believe to keep you in your echo chamber.
- **Intermittent Rewards:** Like a slot machine, you scroll and sometimes get a dopamine jackpot.

Algorithmic Thinking = Less Critical Thinking

The more we let algorithms decide what we see, the more we lose our edge. Our curiosity gets shaped for us. Our outrage gets manufactured. Our worldview narrows.

It's not just content curation. It's thought manipulation.
You weren't meant to be programmable. **You were meant to be present.**

ALGORITHMS DON'T AMPLIFY YOUR VALUES.
THEY EXPLOIT YOUR WEAKNESSES.

Put Pen to Paper:

Reclaiming Your Feed

- **What content types do you want less of?**

☐ Politics ☐ Drama ☐ Celebrity

☐ Fitness pressure ☐ Other:

- **What do you want more of?**

☐ Inspiration ☐ Learning ☐ Calm

☐ Creativity ☐ Other:

Create your “Intentional Algorithm”

- **3 creators that I’ll seek out directly each week:**

1.
2.
3.

- **6 things I will no longer let autoplay decide for me:**

1.
2.
3.
4.
5.
6.

Mental Ad Blockers: Tools, Settings, and Boundaries to Reclaim Control

You can't control every ad or notification. But you can control your exposure, and your response.

Here's the good news: You don't need to move to the woods and smash your phone with a rock. You just need to create intentional friction between you and the hijackers.
Friction = Freedom.

EVERY SCROLL REWIRES YOUR BRAIN.
CHOOSE WHAT YOU LET IN OR SOMEONE ELSE WILL.

Tools to Block the Noise

- **Browser Extensions**
  - Get an extension that can block ads at the root
- **Newsfeed Eradicators**
  - Remove addictive timelines on your social media
- **App Time Limiters**
  - Force intentional entry or block access entirely
- **Built-in native tools**
  - Apple Screen Time (iOS), Digital Wellbeing (Android)
- **Grayscale Mode**
  - Remove color stimulation, instant dopamine diet
- **Notifications Audit**
  - Turn off EVERYTHING that isn't a direct human message

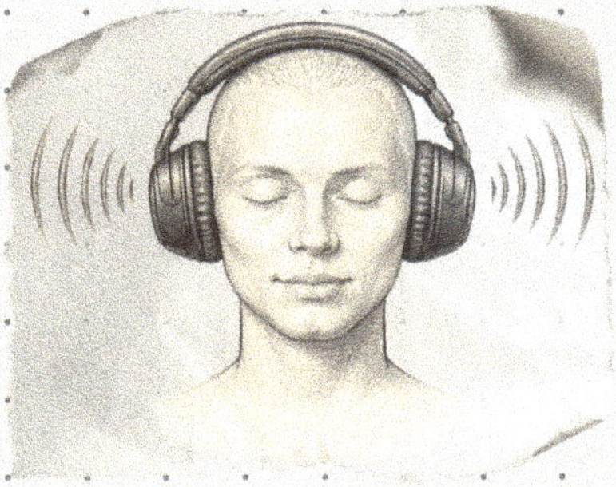

YOU DON'T HAVE A FOCUS PROBLEM.

YOU HAVE AN ENVIRONMENT BUILT TO DESTROY IT, AND A HABIT OF NOT FIGHTING BACK.

Quantum Leap Jumpstart

- Limit social app time to ________ mins per day

STICK TO IT!

- Designate one “Zero Feed Day” per week
  (e.g., no social, no feeds, no doomscrolling)
- Create “no-scroll” zones
  (e.g., the first hour of the day, before bed, during meals)

Put Pen to Paper: Digital Boundary Builder

- **Apps I will delete this week:**

→

- **Apps I will move off my home screen:**

→

- **Notification types I’m turning off now:**

→

- **People I will tell about my digital boundary shift:** (for accountability)

→

Social Media Detox: How to Step Back Without Falling Behind

Let's be honest, most of us don't need social media. We're just afraid of what happens when we're not there.
Afraid we'll miss something. Be forgotten. Feel invisible.

But if it's costing your peace, your focus, your mental clarity, what exactly are you staying visible for?

Disconnecting is not disappearing.
It's reappearing, in your real life.

Social Media Withdrawal Symptoms

- Reflex-checking your phone without a reason
- *"I wonder what I missed?"* anxiety spike
- Urge to share every small thought or meal
- Restlessness in silence, silence feels itchy
- Mindlessly opening apps when your brain goes idle

Nothing's wrong with you.
Your brain is just **deprogramming.**

IF YOU'RE NOT FEEDING YOUR FOCUS,
YOU'RE FEEDING YOUR NUMBNESS.

Detox Strategies That Work

- **7-Day Social Reset**
    - Log out
    - Move the apps off your home screen or into a hidden folder
    - Announce your break to friends or followers so expectations are clear
    - Replace scrolling with journaling or walking

- **Selective Re-entry**
    - After 7 days, reintroduce only what adds value
    - Curate consciously

- **The 3-F Rule: Follow | Filter | Forget**
    - Follow only those who inspire or educate
    - Filter what you see using tools and settings
    - Forget the rest. Mute, unfollow, or delete

- **Digital Sabbath**
    - One full day offline every week with no exceptions

- **Notification Fasting**
    - Turn off all badges, banners, and buzzes
    - Let your mind breathe

YOUR FEED IS YOUR MIRROR: CLEAN IT. CURATE IT. MAKE IT REFLECT WHO YOU WANT TO BECOME.

Put Pen to Paper:

Your Detox Plan

- **Start Date:**

→

- **Platforms I'm stepping away from:**

→

- **What I fear I'll miss:**

→

- **What I hope I'll gain:**

→

- **Activities I'll use to fill that time with real value:**

1.
2.
3.
4.
5.
6.
7.
8.
9.
10.

Reclaiming the Day
Focus. Energy. Drive.

You don't need more hours. You need to get your hours back.

This section isn't about time management. It's about time **liberation.** About taking back what distractions, dopamine loops, and decision fatigue have stolen from you.

It's about remembering who you were before the feed got louder than **your inner voice.**

The 3 Pillars of Daily Clarity

I. Clear Mornings

- Protect the first 60 minutes of your day like your future depends on it

II. Focused Work Blocks

- One task
- One purpose
- One time slot
- No noise

III. Deliberate Transitions

- Create rituals between activities
- A breath
- A stretch
- A walk
- Reset your brain

You don't need more hustle, you need sharper focus.

This is where clarity becomes momentum.
Don't wait for motivation. Build the direction yourself.

If planning ahead and tracking results doesn't resonate with you, you could use a **Task Transition Log.**

This log is for short, timestamped entries that expose reality, not intention. Instead of writing once a day, you log between actions. Each entry captures what just happened, what happens next, and why. This kills unconscious drift and turns your day into measurable data. Over time, it builds a precise Time Audit without guesswork.

Task Transition Log Protocol:

- **Every time you switch tasks, pause for 10–20 seconds and log:**
    - **What you were doing**
    - **What you're about to do**
    - **Why the switch is happening**

That's it.
No story. No reflection. Just truth in motion.

Put Pen to Paper:
Rebuild Your Day

What part of your day feels the most hijacked?
What's one boundary you can place there this week?

- **Name 3 habits that drain your attention:**

1.

2.

3.

- **Name 3 rituals that restore your clarity:**

1.

2.

3.

YOU'RE NOT BEHIND. YOU'RE BURIED.
START DIGGING YOUR WAY BACK TO YOURSELF.

Reclaimed Day Framework

Operational Model: A Day Under Control

Time	Action	Energy Type
6:00 AM	Wake, hydrate, no phone	Presence
6:30 AM	Walk or stretch, journal	Movement + Mind
7:00 AM	Task 1: Important + Urgent	Do it now
7:30 AM	Task 1: Important + Urgent	Do it now
8:00 AM	Drop kids at school	Flow
8:30 AM	Get sunshine	Self-care
9:00 AM	Task 2: Important + Not Urgent	Schedule it
9:30 AM	Task 2: Important + Not Urgent	Schedule it
10:00 AM	Appointments, banks, phone calls	Flow
10:30 AM	Wash clothing, run dishwasher	Flow
11:00 AM	Task 3: Not Important + Urgent	Delegate it
11:30 AM	Task 3: Not Important + Urgent	Delegate it
12:00 PM	Task 3: Not Important + Urgent	Get it done
12:30 PM	Task 4: Not Important + Not Urgent	Delete it
1:00 PM	Lunch without screen	Grounding
1:30 PM	Lunch without screen	Grounding
2:00 PM	Low-pressure task or reflection	Focus
2:30 PM	Walk, rest, music, recharge	Recovery
3:00 PM	Creative expression	Self-care
3:30 PM	Bonus work	Flow
4:00 PM	Break: outdoors, tea, silence	Reset
4:30 PM	Dance class, Yoga, Gym	Self-care
5:00 PM	Social interactions	Mind + Emotions
5:30 PM	TV time, news	Mind
6:00 PM	Family, food, light conversation	Connection
6:30 PM	No screens, slow down	Calm
7:00 PM	Family time, games, read a book	Connection
7:30 PM	Prepare bed, hygiene	Self-care
8:00 PM	Shut down	Recovery

Parts of this framework echo a decision system credited to President Eisenhower. Simple. Brutal. Effective.

Now reclaim your day.
On the next page, schedule the day you want.
Then mark outcomes. Record what survives reality.

Capture your day, or design it. **This is where it becomes real.**

Time	Action	Energy Type
6:00 AM		
6:30 AM		
7:00 AM		
7:30 AM		
8:00 AM		
8:30 AM		
9:00 AM		
9:30 AM		
10:00 AM		
10:30 AM		
11:00 AM		
11:30 AM		
12:00 PM		
12:30 PM		
1:00 PM		
1:30 PM		
2:00 PM		
2:30 PM		
3:00 PM		
3:30 PM		
4:00 PM		
4:30 PM		
5:00 PM		
5:30 PM		
6:00 PM		
6:30 PM		
7:00 PM		
7:30 PM		
8:00 PM		

Record outcomes. Every mark exposes what actually happened to your time.

	FIELD MARKS	MARK DEFINITIONS
✓	**Completed**	Closed loop. Task finished as planned.
✕	**Cancelled**	Ended. Removed from the plan.
→	**Deferred**	Postponed without a new date.
○	**Rescheduled**	Moved to a specific future time or day.
△	**Interrupted**	Started but unfinished. Momentum broken.
★	**Important**	Flagged for priority or extra attention.

- **Field Log [H8] Reflections:**

REALITY CHECK: CHRONOS

DITCH AUTOPILOT NOW!

FIELD LOG	SECTOR I9	SEQ: [09/11]

DITCH AUTOPILOT NOW!

You know that feeling when you get home and can't remember how you got there?
That's not memory loss. That's autopilot.
It's not just about driving. It's how many of us live entire weeks. Wake up, check phone, work, eat, scroll, sleep. Repeat.
This chapter is your call to reclaim the driver's seat. Because no life worth living is built by accident.

We're going to break the loop, question the defaults, and start choosing again, really choosing.

What's Autopilot Living?
Autopilot is when you stop making decisions and start running scripts. It's when your body goes through the motions, but your mind is somewhere else, or nowhere at all.

Here's what it looks like:

- You eat standing up without tasting anything.
- You scroll social media and forget what you just saw.
- You say *"yes"* out of habit, not desire.
- You arrive at the weekend and wonder, *"Where did the week go?"*

You're not lazy. You're not broken.
You're overstimulated and under-questioned.

Signs You're Running on Autopilot

- You check your phone before your feet hit the floor in the morning
- You "reward" stress with food or scrolling on autopilot
- You feel like life is happening to you, not through you
- Your calendar is full, but your soul feels empty

Let's get out of the trance.

Why We Default to Autopilot

- **Decision Fatigue:** Too many choices. Not enough clarity.
- **Cultural Programming:** *"This is just how it's done."*
- **Avoidance of Discomfort:** Numbing out > facing truth
- **Overwhelm:** When everything feels urgent, we retreat into the familiar.

But here's the truth: Every system will push you to sleepwalk through life. Every ad. Every platform. Every outdated expectation.
You can't escape the loop until you name it.

Put Pen to Paper:

The Autopilot Audit

Step 1: Where are you most likely to go on autopilot?

- ☐ Mornings
- ☐ Evenings
- ☐ Work routines
- ☐ Meals
- ☐ Weekends
- ☐ Relationships

Step 2: What's your most common default loop? Describe the pattern:

→

Step 3: How does it make you feel?

- ☐ Disconnected
- ☐ Distracted
- ☐ Numb
- ☐ Safe but stuck
- ☐ Busy but unfulfilled

- **What's one moment you can interrupt the cycle tomorrow?**

→

Every moment is a portal. **Choose to step through it awake.**

Interrupting the Loop: Real-Time Pattern Breaks

So you've identified your autopilot moments.
Now what?
You don't need a total life overhaul. You need **micro-interruptions.**
Just enough awareness to steer the wheel instead of letting the script run your day.

Micro-interruptions: small, intentional pattern breaks that pull you out of autopilot before momentum locks in.
Micro-interruptions are the smallest unit of conscious living.

Here's how to do it:

- **Name the loop:** Catch the moment it begins.
(*"This is the part where I scroll for 40 minutes."*)

- **Breathe or move:** A physical state change disrupts mental inertia.

- **Insert choice:** Ask, *"What do I actually want right now?"* Then **act.**

AUTOPILOT IS SAFE. CONSCIOUS LIVING IS BRAVE.

Kindness as a Pattern Interrupt

Sometimes the fastest way out of your fog is to shift the spotlight. When you're spiraling inward, look outward. Kindness pulls you back into the present.

Kindness is a superpower. It restores connection. It creates purpose. It multiplies energy. And you don't need a grand gesture. You just need to disrupt your day with a small spark of humanity.

Acts of Kindness That Interrupt

- Pick up trash at the beach or park
- Leave a positive comment on someone's post
- Write a handwritten thank-you note
- Let someone cut in line without resentment
- Compliment a stranger genuinely
- Text a friend just to remind them they matter
- Tip extra if you can afford it
- Donate one item you never use to someone who needs it
- Offer to help a neighbor with yardwork or errands
- Smile at five people in a row without expecting anything back

These small actions are like **emotional CPR**. They reset you and ripple outward.

SOMETIMES THE BEST WAY TO RECONNECT WITH YOURSELF IS TO SHOW UP FOR SOMEONE ELSE.

Put Pen to Paper:

Kindness Disruptor List

- What act of kindness could you do in the next 10 minutes?

→

- What weekly kindness ritual could you build into your life?

→

- Who in your life could use a little more of your presence or appreciation?

→

Building New Conscious Habits: Make the Shift Stick

You've interrupted the pattern. Now it's time to replace it.

Because here's the truth: If you remove a behavior and don't replace it, the old pattern comes back stronger.

Don't just subtract. **Substitute.**

The Conscious Habit Formula

The C.A.R. method: Cue → Action → Reward

C: Anchor your habit to something that already happens.

A: Make it short, simple, and satisfying.

R: Acknowledge it. Feel good about doing it.

Example:

C: *Brush teeth*

A: *60 seconds of breathwork*

R: *Notice your body unclenching. This is what being here feels like.*

The goal isn't perfection. It's **consistency.**
Start with habits that feel like relief, not punishment.

PATTERN + AWARENESS = CONTROL OF YOUR NEXT MOVE.

[Inspired by classic habit loop research, adapted for practical use]

Put Pen to Paper:

Conscious Habit Map

Cue (What it follows)	Action (Habit I'm building)	Reward (Feeling It Brings)

Building New Conscious Habits: Make the Shift Stick

- **Now stack it into your day:**
  - **Morning:**

→

  - **Midday:**

→

  - **Evening:**

→

Disable Autopilot: Design Your Environment

You can't rely on willpower. It's not designed for long-haul resistance. But your environment? That's a powerful ally.
Make your space remind you who you want to be, not who you've been on autopilot.

Environmental Cues That Shape You

- Phone out of reach → **more presence**
- Journal by your bed → **more reflection**
- Guitar not in the closet → **more creativity**
- Water bottle within reach → **more hydration**
- Books visible, not stacked away → **more curiosity**

Put Pen to Paper: Space Reboot Blueprint

- **What space in your home feels most like an autopilot zone?**

→

- **What items live there that keep old patterns alive?**

→

- **What 3 objects or cues could you add or move to change that space's energy?**

1.
2.
3.

- **What's one thing you can remove this week to make space for clarity?**

→

The Daily Disruptor Ritual: Reset Your Mind on Purpose

You can't think your way into a new life. **You have to act your way into it:** repeatedly, intentionally, until it becomes your new normal.

This ritual isn't complicated. It's a mini reboot you run every single day to interrupt the noise and **choose presence.**

YOUR LIFE ALREADY HAS RITUALS.

MAKE SURE THEY SERVE WHO YOU'RE BECOMING.

The Daily Disruptor

I. **One-Minute Grounding:**
   - Sit
   - Breathe
   - Feel your body.
   - No tech. No input.

II. **One Bold Question:**
   - Ask, *"What matters most today?"*

→

III. **One Chosen Act:**
   - Pick one thing, habit, kindness, movement, focus, and do it like it means something. **Because it does.**

That's it. **Simple. Repeatable. Transformational.**

- **What other daily disruptors can you deploy?**

→

- **Quick Reflection:**

LET YOUR HABITS DO THE HEAVY LIFTING.
ARCHITECT YOUR NEXT LEVEL.

Put Pen to Paper:

Build Your Disruptor

- Where in your day could you add this disruptor?
  - Morning:

→

  - Midday:

→

  - Evening:

→

- What location would anchor it?
  (e.g., the desk, patio, car, kitchen floor)

→

- What reminder can you set to make it stick?

→

Quantum Leap Jumpstart

Design your version:

- **My 1-minute anchor:**

→

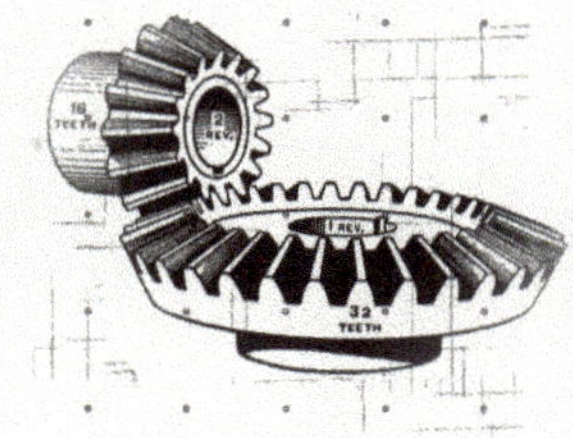

- **My go-to bold question:**

→

- **My signature disruptor move:**

→

You don't need a 3-hour routine. You need one grounded moment of **full presence.**
Do this daily and watch your life sharpen, one **awake** minute at a time.

YOUR ENVIRONMENT WHISPERS TO YOUR SUBCONSCIOUS ALL DAY.

CHANGE WHAT IT SAYS.

- **Field Log [I9] Reflections:**

REALITY CHECK: CHRONOS

AUTHOR YOUR OWN ENDING

FIELD LOG	SECTOR J10	SEQ: [10/11]

AUTHOR YOUR OWN ENDING

You've taken the audit. You've interrupted the noise.
Now it's time to write something worth living.

This chapter is about authorship. Your life is already being written, whether you realize it or not.
Every choice. Every yes. Every ignored instinct. Every brave disruption. Every pattern you broke, and every one you didn't.

The only question is: Are you writing it on purpose?

You're not just the main character. You're the writer, director, and editor.

This is where you build your storyboard. One that reflects who you want to be, not just what you've been told to pursue.
This is about aligning your time with your values, Your time aligns with your values. Your energy aligns with your purpose. Your story aligns with your truth.

The Plot Twist: You Get to Choose.

Most people live like their life was assigned. As if their job, habits, and lifestyle were handed down from some invisible committee. But you? You know better now.

The real power isn't in knowing what to do. It's in choosing what to do **next**.

You're standing in a new scene. Pen in hand. It's time to choose your direction. Your values. Your rhythm. Your future.
And you don't need to rewrite your entire story overnight. Just the next paragraph.

Life Blueprint

A contract with your future self.
Personal. Flexible. Alive.

Write it. Then commit to seeing it through.

Put Pen to Paper: Map the Core Themes of Your Story

Step 1:

- **What are your core themes?** Every great story has recurring themes. Love, growth, justice, resilience, joy, clarity.

- **What are yours?**

→

Now ask: Are your days filled with actions that reflect those themes? If not, it's time to revise the plot.

- **Quick Reflection:**

Step 2:

- **Who's in your cast?** Stories need characters. So does your life. But not everyone gets to be in your main storyline.

- **Who are your core 5 people?**

1.
2.
3.
4.
5.

- **Who needs to be moved to the background?**

→

- **Who are you still trying to impress that doesn't matter?**

→

- **Write the names that stay:**

→

THE PEOPLE YOU KEEP SHAPE THE WORLD YOU LIVE IN.

- **Who gets less access from now on?**

→

SOME PEOPLE SHOULD ONLY GET TO SEE YOU ONCE A YEAR.

Time Allocation = Storytelling

You can tell me what you care about, but if I look at how you spend your time, I'll know the truth. Time is your narrator. It reveals your values, even when your words say otherwise.

Show me your calendar and I'll show you your story. This is not about hustle. It's about intention. It's about realizing that **every hour** you spend is a line in the autobiography of the life you're actively writing.

Put Pen to Paper:

Time Reflection Exercise

Let's take inventory of the hours that are writing your story:

Category	Hours/Week	Is This Story-Aligned?	Adjustments Needed?
sleep		□ YES □ NO	□ YES □ NO
work		□ YES □ NO	□ YES □ NO
commuting		□ YES □ NO	□ YES □ NO
eating/cooking		□ YES □ NO	□ YES □ NO
scrolling/TV/content		□ YES □ NO	□ YES □ NO
movement/exercise		□ YES □ NO	□ YES □ NO
family/friends		□ YES □ NO	□ YES □ NO
learning/reading		□ YES □ NO	□ YES □ NO
creative/hobbies		□ YES □ NO	□ YES □ NO
silence/reflection		□ YES □ NO	□ YES □ NO
connection/intimacy		□ YES □ NO	□ YES □ NO
mental health		□ YES □ NO	□ YES □ NO

- **What's missing?**

→

- **What's taking up too much room?**

→

Defining Your Legacy Without Waiting to Die

Let's be clear about something: legacy isn't about statues or eulogies. It's about impact, what echoes after your presence.
You don't have to be gone for your legacy to begin. In fact, **it already has.**

Legacy is built in the tiny moments most people rush past.

It's how you show up for people. What you choose to create. The energy you leave in a room after you leave it.

You're writing your ending now, every day.

YOUR LIFE IS NOT A TO-DO LIST. IT'S A STORY ARC

MAKE SURE THE PACING MATCHES THE PLOT YOU WANT.

Quantum Leap Jumpstart

- What are the 3 qualities I hope people remember about me?

1.
2.
3.

- What would I want my kids/friends/partner/team to say about me right now, not someday?

→

- What's one habit I can commit to this week that builds the legacy I want to leave?

→

- If I vanished tomorrow, what unfinished message or project would I regret leaving undone?

→

Now reframe that as your **top priority.**

LEGACY ISN'T WHAT YOU LEAVE BEHIND;
IT'S WHAT YOU LIVE OUT LOUD WHILE YOU'RE HERE.

MAKE IT SOMETHING YOU'RE PROUD TO ECHO FORWARD.

Crafting Your Final Reality Check Plan

You've done the audit. You've rewritten your plot. You've aligned your time. You've started to live your **legacy.**

Now it's time to lock it in with your **Final Reality Check Plan**, a living document for how you'll show up, decide, and design the rest of your days.

This isn't a to-do list. It's a **life-intention blueprint.**

A declaration that says:
"This is who I am, and this is what I will no longer tolerate or postpone."

The Final 5: Core Commitments to Yourself

I. I will no longer waste my Life-Hours on:

→

II. I will invest more presence and energy into:

→

III. I will protect my clarity by eliminating:

→

IV. I will give myself permission to:

→

V. I will live by this core rule:

→

Visualize the Future You're Choosing

Write it out like it's already happening:
(e.g., "I wake up and…" "My time flows like…" "My impact is seen in…")

- **How does your ideal day feel?**

→

- **What does your environment look like?**

→

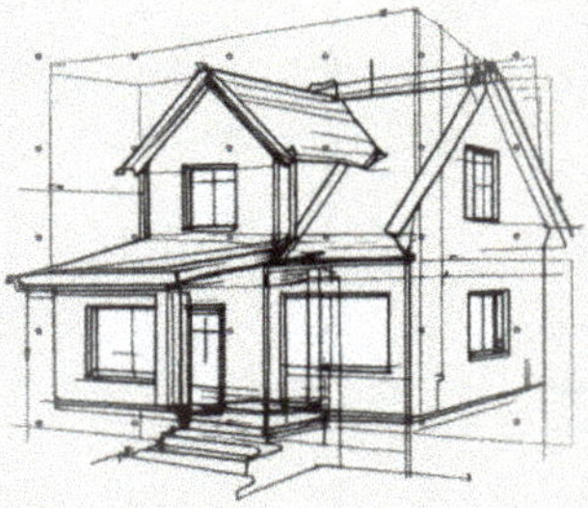

- **Who's around you?**

→

YOU DON'T NEED TO LIVE FOREVER.
YOU JUST NEED TO LIVE FULLY WHILE YOU'RE HERE.

- **What are you building, learning, contributing?**

→

- **What energy do you carry with you?**

→

This is not fantasy. **It's direction.**

Final Words for the Author of This Life

There will still be distractions. There will still be pressure. But now, there will also be **intention**.

You are the author. You get to revise at any time. You are allowed to pivot, to evolve, to say "*this chapter is over.*"
You are allowed to dream again.

So **do it.**

WRITE THE ENDING
THAT LEAVES NO DOUBT
YOU WERE HERE.

- **Field Log [J10] Reflections:**

REALITY CHECK: CHRONOS

YOUR FINAL REALITY CHECK

FIELD LOG	SECTOR K11	SEQ: [11/11]

YOUR FINAL REALITY CHECK

Let's not dance around it. You are going to die. So am I.
And when that moment comes, when your final day arrives, you will take nothing with you. Not the house. Not the car. Not the shoes, gadgets, trophies, or the dozens of things you bought because an ad told you they would make you whole.

And here's what's wild: most of the people you spent your life trying to impress? They'll forget you in a few weeks. Life will move on without you in it.
That's not depressing. That's **liberating.**

It means you can stop performing. Stop chasing applause you won't even hear. Stop wasting your Life-Hours on things that won't even be remembered.

This chapter is your **exhale.** Your **reset.** It's the moment you get clear on what actually matters.

And it's your last reminder:
Make the time you have left feel like it belongs to **you.**

The Great Unburdening

Here's something else to consider:
When you die, you won't just leave behind your possessions. You'll also leave behind your fears. Your insecurities. Your regrets. Your unspoken apologies. Your childhood wounds. **None of it comes with you.**

The weight you're carrying? It's temporary. And most of it was never yours to begin with.

That means you can start letting go now. You can stop punishing yourself for mistakes already paid for in tears and time. You can stop running from fears that, if we're honest, are mostly fiction.

Here's a wild truth: The majority of what you fear will never happen. And the things that *do* happen? You'll survive them. You already have.

Fear is a brilliant actor. A convincing voice. **Fear is a liar.** READ THAT AGAIN!

You don't have to carry it into every room. You don't have to keep dragging your past into every tomorrow.

So pause here. **Breathe.** Forgive yourself for not knowing better. And choose, from this page forward, to travel **lighter**.

- **Quick Reflection:**

The Life-Hour Countdown (One Last Time)

Let's return to the numbers, one final, sobering time. Not to scare you. To focus you.

You only have a set number of hours left in this world. [025]

You get the idea: the usable time is shrinking.
But it's not too late.
It's never too late.

Every single one of those hours is a chance to:

- Reconnect with someone who matters
- Act on what you've been postponing
- Create something that outlasts you
- Heal something that's been festering
- Sit still and savor the damn sky

You don't need to "buy time." You need to claim the time you already have and **own it.**

This final audit isn't about mortality. It's about urgency with purpose. **Make the rest count.**

Quantum Leap Jumpstart

This is your last quantum leap. The one that echoes.

You've stared at the numbers. You've seen through the illusions. You've remembered that none of the fear, stuff, or status comes with you.

So now ask yourself: What will you do with the time left?

Not someday. Not when things calm down. Not after the next raise, move, relationship, or vacation.
Now.

The Reality Check Contract

This is the final reality check:

- What are you done pretending to care about?
- What dream or value have you kept on the back burner?
- What are you no longer available for?
- What version of you are you finally ready to step into, fully, unapologetically?

This is not a dress rehearsal. You don't need another productivity app or a better planner. **You need bold alignment.**

You need to mean it when you say:
"This is my life. And I'm going to live it like it matters."

Fill this in. Make it yours. Post it. Revisit it.

Today, I commit to:

→

I will no longer waste time on:

→

I will forgive myself for:

→

I will say yes to:

→

I will be remembered for:

→

Breathe. Step forward. It's your time.

And the reality check? Most of us won't make it to 100.
But we do choose the story we write with the time we've got left.

Live like you matter, and watch your life rise to meet you.

You rewrote yourself in the margins of this field guide.

Treat it like a boundary. A blueprint. A new operating system.

You are not the same person who started this. You walked through the fire and took back your time.

REALITY CHECK: CHRONOS / COMPLETED

FINISHED ON:

- **Field Log [K11] Reflections:**

- **Reality Check: CHRONOS Reflections:**

You've reclaimed your time. Now look up.

Reality Check: CHRONOS is not about doing more.
It is about seeing clearly.

How your time is spent.
What it costs you.
What it gives back.

Not in theory.
In practice.

More than a field guide.
It's a life audit in your hands.

What you do with that clarity is now yours to decide.

→ See your real Life-Hour wage
→ Notice where time, energy, and attention leak
→ Question the defaults you follow
→ Shape a life that actually feels like yours

C. T. Jovenich works at the intersection of psychology, business, and human behavior, questioning how we measure value and move through life.

An entrepreneur and strategist, his work cuts through illusions and turns insight into tools you can use to see clearly, decide differently, and **act with intention.**

Known for a direct, unfiltered voice, he leans into the questions most people avoid, inviting readers to examine how their time and choices are shaping their lives.

He lives in the Inland Empire, California with his wife, 3 kids, 2 dogs, 3 cats, 7 chickens, and 3 koi fish.

This is an audit of your hours, choices, emotions, and direction.

Time is the currency.
You are the investment.

The return is decided by what you do next.

Begin.

CONTINUE WHEN YOU'RE READY

JOVENICHBOOKS.COM

www.ingramcontent.com/pod-product-compliance
Lightning Source LLC
Chambersburg PA
CBHW041800220926
51847CB00014B/272
* 9 7 8 1 9 7 0 2 8 5 0 0 0 *